OUT OF OFFICE

ABOUT THE AUTHOR

 Fiona Thomas is a freelance writer who was born in Glasgow but is now living in Birmingham, UK. She has been published in *Metro*, *Reader's Digest*, *Happiful Magazine* and *Grazia*. Her passion is working with female-led businesses and shining a light on the positive impact that freelancing can have on our wellbeing. This is her second book.

OUT OF OFFICE

By Fiona Thomas

TRIGGER
The mental health & wellbeing publisher

First published in 2020
This edition published in 2023 by Trigger Publishing
An imprint of Shaw Callaghan Ltd

UK Office
The Stanley Building
7 Pancras Square
Kings Cross
London N1C 4AG

US Office
On Point Executive Center, Inc
3030 N Rocky Point Drive W
Suite 150
Tampa, FL 33607
www.triggerhub.org

A CIP catalogue record for this book is available upon request from the British Library
ISBN: 978-1-83796-288-4
Ebook ISBN: 978-1-83796-289-1

Cover design by Bookollective
Typeset by Lapiz Digital Services

DEDICATION

For all the self-doubters. You got this.

FOREWORD

Self-employment has made me unemployable. Perhaps that's a slightly odd sentence to be opening a book on self-employment with, but I've come to consider this to be a Very Good Thing in my life. Working for myself has changed me so completely — broadened my mind and my skill set so far beyond what I believed was possible — that the only company I can imagine myself ever choosing to work at in future is one that I have lovingly built for myself.

The 9-5 world is one-size-fits-all. It's seems to me that it's built for a prototype human who's always active, always productive, never sick, not menstruating, nor crying in the loos over some personal strife. It requires us to check our humanity at the door for around nine hours a day, and when we struggle to do this, it tells us the problem is us.

As somebody with a chronic health condition and ADHD, it's little wonder I felt like a jaggedy star-shaped peg being jammed into that round workplace hole. Going freelance felt like my chance to run for the hills, and I snatched at it with tired and work-worn hands.

The reality was less romantic. Faced with my first day in The Land of No Payday, I did what all digital freelancers do in a time of quandary: I logged in to Twitter. Five years later, I still remember word for word, some of the beautiful messages I got in response to my fears.

It was Twitter that introduced me to Fiona. I can't recall how I first found her, exactly: it could have been through our overlapping circles of mental health conversations, the blogging world, Intuitive Eating or perhaps one of her #journorequests, which always seemed to be describing me. However it happened, I recognised her immediately as a buoyancy aid in the choppy seas of self-employed life. She was someone with enough optimism to keep both of our heads above water, and her no-bullshit attitude would help us to steer clear of the sharks.

They were right, those jolly Twitter commenters. This was easily going to turn out to be the best choice of my life, but it was also one of the hardest. Support for freelancers is way behind the curve, and I speak daily to creatives and business owners still miserably mired in the midst of impenetrable tax legislation, lost in the perpetual loop of government advice websites or simply struggling to get out of their pyjamas.

I suppose this is why I've come to see running your own business as a trial-by-fire type of therapy. (That's not, btw, to suggest conventional professional therapy isn't still a tremendous investment. I'm a huge advocate, and believe every human can benefit from it.) Self-employment calls on us to come face to face with many things we've avoided previously. It means showing up, being seen, speaking out and actively selling ourselves... seeing the value in our time and in what we do in the world, all while keeping enough conviction in that belief to be able to ask others to believe in it too. We have to unpack our money baggage and our attitudes to work and creativity. It took me three solid years of at-home self-employment before I could finally accept that the hours spent reading or gazing out of a window were as essential to my output as the time spent bathing in the blue light of my laptop. Nobody teaches this stuff, and it's hard to navigate all on your own... until now.

This book is the straight-talking life raft that I would have happily clung to in those turbulent first years. It's a shortcut to the most hard-won realisations every freelancer comes to, and a generous sharing of the nitty-gritty stuff in between. *"Work isn't meant to be fun,"* my dad used to tell me. *"That's why they call it work."* But what if it could be? What if it was meant to be, all along? What self-employment has taught me, above all else, is to place a much higher value on all my hours: the ones spent working, and those devoted to family and friends... as well as the ones wisely invested in reading books such as this, to really equip me to get the very best out of my time.

I've learned that my wellbeing and happiness is worth more than the minimum wage, and I believe yours should be too. Forget being the worker bee. Read on, my friend — because it's time to become your own queen.

Sara Tasker, bestselling author and business coach
www.meandorla.co.uk

CONTENTS

GLOSSARY

This book is by no means a complicated piece of literature, but it will feature a few freelancing terms that you may not have come across before.

Most of them are explained in detail at some point in the book, but if you forget ('cause let's be honest, we all zone out occasionally), you can refer back to these definitions:

Client: the individual or business who pays for your product or services

Co-working: working with other freelancers in a shared space

Contract: formal agreement between two parties, e.g. freelancer and client

Income tax: tax paid to the government based on your earnings

Invoice: a document sent to the client in order to obtain payment for goods or services provided

Outsourcing: hiring a professional to complete tasks that you are unable or too busy to do yourself

Rates: how much you charge the client for your product or services

Side hustle: a passion project that is undertaken outside of your regular day job

Sole trader: the term used when someone is the sole business owner, entitled to keep all profits after tax has been paid, but also liable for all losses

INTRODUCTION

Before you get stuck into this gem of a book, I want to fill you in on a few minor details.

ONE.

My personality dictates that I have a strong negative bias towards myself. That's cool. Whatever. Basically, I lie awake at night and worry that people are going to pick up this book, hate it, feel incredibly disappointed and leave me horrible Amazon reviews, which will, of course, confirm my negative thoughts and make me a bit sad. In a bid to counteract this fear I have decided to include this disclaimer section along with advice on how to read this book.

TWO.

I was born in Scotland and currently live and work in Birmingham, UK. Any laws or business talk are firmly rooted in my experience working in this country, but don't let that put you off. Freelancing is popular across the globe and this book answers questions and offers tips that are applicable to people everywhere. I'm registered as a sole trader, but 99% of what I talk about in this book is applicable to anyone who works for themselves in some capacity. Whichever term you use (freelancer, business owner, 'mompreneur'), this book is designed to help you attain and enjoy a career out of office, on your own terms.

THREE.

I am white. I am child-free. I am married. I come from a stable family life. I'm not saying I haven't suffered in life (my first book, *Depression in a Digital Age*, explains my history with mental illness in more detail if you're interested), but I'm aware that my personal circumstances have made a freelancing career easier than it might be for others. Although I believe that freelancing is accessible to anyone, that doesn't mean it's easy.

FOUR.

This is not a book on how to make a quick buck. Or even a slow buck. Not even a medium-rare buck. I didn't get into freelancing to make more money (but if you did, that's cool, no judgement) but I do know that money is essential to survival. I talk a lot about how to make enough money to suit your needs, how to set rates and get paid, but you probably won't make your first million after reading my words. If you do, you should definitely mention that in your Amazon review.

FIVE.

This book doesn't require you to read it from start to finish. Flick through and see what takes your fancy. If you're starting out as a freelancer or even just flirting with the idea, start with Part One. That's where I'll chat about your mindset and what it takes to make the leap. If you've already been freelancing for a while or have some specific questions that need an answer, then head to Part Two. That's where I'll cover the technical aspects such as contracts, how to pay tax, claim expenses and what kind of insurance you might want to think about. Once you've got the ball rolling, you might be ready to tweak a few things to level up your business. If this is the case, dive right into Part Three. That's where I'll help you fine-tune your freelance lifestyle to make sure you continue to live a life that's happy, productive and full of potential. If you're currently wiping a three-day-old guacamole stain off your pyjamas and wondering whether you'll have time to shower this week, skip to Part Four, stat. That's where you'll find a few friendly reminders on how to take care of your mental and physical self, manage burnout and take a holiday once in a while.

I would encourage you to highlight my inspiring words (did I mention I'm super humble?) to refer to in times of crisis. Fold down corners on the pages that really speak to you. If you come up with an idea of your own, write it in the margins. Scribble away. Deface this book. That's an order.

Now, let's get on with this, shall we?

PART ONE

GETTING THE SHOW ON THE ROAD

CHAPTER 1

WTF IS FREELANCING?

FREELANCE[1]

adverb
BrE /ˈfriːlɑːns/; NAmE /ˈfriːlæns/
(especially British English)
by selling your work or services to several different
organisations rather than being employed by one particular
organisation
   Example:

- I work freelance from home.
- She went (= started to work) freelance last year.

When you book time off work to jump on a plane to
Ibiza or have a messy hen weekend in Blackpool, there
is nothing more satisfying than setting your 'out of
office' email response. Along with spending a full ninety
minutes perusing the miniature toiletries section at the
beauty counter, clicking 'save' on that out-of-office reply
is a rare and delicious moment. One to be savoured a

Basically, a helluvalotta people are jumping ship and getting that OOO feeling.

handful of times per year. It's almost definitely followed by a smug exit, a subtle flick of the hair and a deep breath of relaxation as you internally say *F**k You* to the office space that you normally inhabit for thirty-seven hours per week. But imagine if that out-of-office feeling (or that 'OOO' feeling as I like to call it) was achievable on a more permanent basis. What if you could really say *F**k You* to office life?

Well, the reality is that many of us already have. Freelancing is booming. The 2019 Freelancing in America study[2] found that there were 57 million freelancers in the US alone. In the same year, data showed there were 4.8 million of us in the UK. Countries such as Brazil, Pakistan and Ukraine have also seen a significant increase in the number of people working on a freelance basis.[3] Basically, a helluvalotta people are jumping ship and getting that OOO feeling.

Everyone has probably freelanced at some point, even if they didn't realise it at the time. Have you ever sold off an extra gig ticket and made some profit from the transaction? Held a car boot sale to offload your old junk in exchange for hard cash? Been asked to walk someone's dog or feed their cat for a tenner? You've freelanced! It feels good, right? Getting to choose the work you do, be your own boss and get paid in return is awesome. When you think about it this way, it's not that scary (unless you hate animals of course), and it's pretty accessible too. Some people refer to freelancing as self-employment. Others talk about the gig economy, and some freelancers call themselves business owners.

I go between labelling myself as both freelance and self-employed, and I use both of these terms throughout this book. Forgive me if it doesn't sit well with you; just know that my intention is to make us all feel part of the same community, even if we use different names for what we do.

The term 'freelancer' comes with negative connotations. There, I've said it. People think that freelancers float around from job to job with no direction in life and certainly no company loyalty. I've spoken to successful freelancers who prefer to call themselves consultants or executives because it gets them meetings with the right people. Some big brands (or the people behind them) turn their noses up at freelancers, so bear that in mind when you describe your services to potential clients. Me? I'm proud to be a freelancer.

STATE OF AFFAIRS

Here are some interesting figures:

- The ONS stated that the number of UK self-employed workers aged 16–24 has almost doubled since 2001
- According to data from Upwork, 59% of US companies are now using remote workers or freelancers
- The same report says that 53% of US freelancers are Gen Z (aged 23–38)

(BTW, I'm writing in 2020, so if you're reading this book in the future and want up-to-date figures, then google it.

Or command your friendly robot butler to do it for you. It depends exactly how far in the future we're talking here.)

IS IT A GIRL THANG?

I surround myself with female friends, many of whom are freelancers. For a while that firmly implanted the bias in my head that freelancers are mostly women, but, of course, this isn't true at all. Globally the ratio of female freelancers is less than a quarter (23%), with male workers holding the majority (77%).[4] But this differs depending on location; in the UK, for example, the female percentage is 41% compared to 59% male.[5]

As a woman it's easy for me to rhyme off the discrimination that we face in the workplace because I lived it for many years. I saw colleagues instructed to wear makeup and opt for shorter skirts to please male customers. Others chose to hide their engagement ring to be in with a chance of a promotion. But the truth is that men are routinely discriminated against in the world of work too. They are often denied flexible working requests, not promoted because they have kids, or simply not hired for roles that are considered 'women's work'.

Male or female, freelancing can help people take back some of the control that is lost in the traditional work environment. Out of office, there is no need to explain to clients that you have children or hide your wedding band. When you work remotely, clients may never even see your face, so they can't judge you on how pretty your hair is or what clothes you wear. Generally speaking, all business is conducted on the basis of your ability to deliver the work with no need to discuss personal details.

WORKING MUMS

An IPSE report[6] shows that the number of UK new mums choosing to go freelance instead of returning to full-time office work post-baby has gone up by 79% since 2008. I'm not a parent myself, but I can see exactly why so many mothers are turning to the world of freelance through necessity, rather than choice.

I've heard numerous tales about new mums being blocked out of work emails, given the cold shoulder, left out of key decisions, made redundant or losing their job due to conveniently timed 'restructuring'. A report by the National Women's Law Center and A Better Balance[7] opens with the following comment on the current climate for pregnant women in the USA: 'Despite the Pregnancy Discrimination Act's protections, pregnant workers' requests are often denied – leaving many pregnant women without a salary because they are forced to quit, are fired, or are pushed out onto unpaid leave.'

In the UK, it is estimated that 54,000 women[8] lose their job during pregnancy or motherhood, and with only a three-month window available to file a claim, it's no wonder that looking after a newborn and hunting for a new job take precedence over fighting their ill-treatment.

Although logistics play a big part in mums in particular going freelance, it's worth pointing out that it's also an important way for many to reclaim their identities when they feel shunned by the traditional workplace.

Take Mikhila McDaid for example. The thirty-two-year-old mother of two, content creator and author of *Life Styling: Simple Steps for Mums to Find Style and Confidence* told me the impact her business has had on her state of mind:

I had my daughter when I was nineteen so I didn't have a moment to consider what I wanted my life to be before it was all about her. I'm not ambitious so I never imagined that work would fulfil me in any significant way but having my little corner of the internet, blogging and vlogging gave me a new source of self-esteem as well as massively diluting any longing I could have for a life unlived.

That's not to say we should ignore the harsh realities at play here. In a Refinery29 article entitled 'Work Isn't Working: The Real Reason More Women Are Going Freelance', Anna Codrea-Rado says that women often make the difficult decision to go freelance even though it can carry a financial burden:

On the face of it … freelancing gives working mothers the control they need to have a fulfilling family and professional life. It's a boon for female empowerment. Except there's an uncomfortable truth lurking here as well: women would rather put themselves in a vulnerable financial position than have to put up with the dissatisfaction of working in traditional employment.[9]

Which leads us nicely on to…

THE MONEY ASPECT

I really admire people who are financially driven because I think it makes life a lot simpler. Me, I'm creatively driven, and while that fills up my cup, it doesn't pay the bills. From the outset, it might look like freelancers make a lot of money. For example, I can make £300 for a twenty-minute speaking gig, but that doesn't mean I make £900 an hour. Far from it in fact.

You may be tempted to go it alone after doing a few pieces of work in tandem with your day job, but bear in mind that you won't make that money consistently. There will be droughts. There will be tumbleweed. There will be long stretches of nothingness in between the odd eye-wateringly generous fee.

Some of the top-paying freelance roles in 2019 were identified as quantity surveyor, artist, graphic designer, recruiter and therapist,[10] so if you're in any of these industries then you're in good shape. The 2019 Freelancing in America Study[11] found that the median rate for the country's freelancers is $20 per hour (the US overall is just $18.80) and those offering skilled services have a higher median rate of $28 per hour. In the UK, however, data suggests that freelancers are earning less than those who are traditionally employed, earning an average of £240 a week (compared to employees, who earn around £400 in the same time frame[12]). However, these figures don't take into account the fact that many freelancers need less money when they work from home (perhaps as a result of no commuting costs or reduced childcare needs), or the fact that many freelancers choose to work on a part-time basis instead of full-time, so they should be taken with a pinch of salt.

DITCHING THE 9-TO-5

The 2019 Global Workspace Survey revealed that 75% of workers want the option for flexible working and consider this to be the 'new normal'.[13] Research from YouGov Omnibus[14] reveals that, given the choice, two thirds (66%) of working Britons would prefer their eight-hour work day to start and finish earlier.

Thankfully, some companies have cottoned on to the fact that ditching the 9-to-5 model can actually help them retain employees. One study conducted on behalf of McDonald's found that flexible workers reported that they were 'more motivated, and it encouraged them to stay in a job for longer'[15] whilst another survey found that 85% of respondents saw an increase in productivity as a result of greater flexibility.[16]

Lots of companies are trying to create that out of office vibe *in* the office. One such technique was implemented by Jody Thompson and Cali Ressler, where employees are paid based on their output as opposed to the number of hours they've worked. This 'Results-Only Work Environment' (ROWE) is said to decrease staff turnover while improving employee productivity, engagement and satisfaction.[17]

Companies such as Netflix and Evernote are rumoured to offer an unlimited vacation policy (yes please!) to keep staff happy, while others encourage job-sharing and flexible deadlines. In an interview with CNBC, Upwork CEO Stephane Kasriel said that it's just a matter of time before remote working tips over into the mainstream, with baby boomers retiring and Gen X moving into leadership roles. He explains:

Younger generations will see the trade-offs in quality of life and think traditional models are ridiculous. This is similar to how digital natives changed the way we use technology. As younger generations take management reins, remote-work and flexible-work models will just be the norm to them. They'll hire more remote people and empower their teams to work that way.[18]

Okay, so the boring office set-up stinks, but what exactly is it about freelancing that feels so good? Why are future generations expected to be working out of office? I've already touched on some of the reasons women feel freelancing is the best way to earn a living, but why else are so many of us (male or female) attracted to going solo, regardless of the risk?

CHAPTER 2

THE BENEFITS OF FREELANCING

Like any big career change, there are pros and cons to going freelance. I'll definitely get into the negative aspects of freelancing later, but, for now, let's look at the host of benefits that could potentially outweigh the risks of becoming self-employed.

A SENSE OF FREEDOM

Do you feel like the rules and regulations imposed at work are making you feel stifled? It's not in your head. There are lots of people out there secretly dreaming of solitude as they jaunt into work each day, psyching themselves up to act like a 'team player'. In fact, a 2017 study by researchers at the University of Birmingham in the UK concluded that autonomy at work can lead to greater job satisfaction and reported levels of wellbeing.[19]

Basically, having to work around red tape or within specific boundaries can make us feel like crap. Most of the time we just want to be trusted to carry out tasks to the best of our ability in our own time, in a way that suits us. The research found that control over our own schedule is a highly sought-after benefit and helps us truly enjoy our work.

Some people just can't thrive in a traditional work environment. Whether through circumstances or just personal preference, many of us need a sense of independence that isn't achievable in a regular job. Some of us want to watch daytime television and work in the evenings. Others work best at 5 am and then head to the gym at midday. Or maybe you're like me and purposely book a four-hour train journey to Scotland because you know you'll have zero distractions and will finally get started on chapter one of your book.

It's not all about productivity, either. Maybe you want to be the decision-maker for once, or you want to see a project through from start to finish with full creative control. Maybe you want financial freedom, the ability to bank your yearly salary by July and take the rest of the year off to work on your stand-up routine or help build a hospital in Africa. The point is, it's up to *you*.

JOB SECURITY

Have you heard about the freelancer who made herself redundant? Of course you haven't, because it's literally (er, let's say probably) never happened. Being your own boss means that as long as you have paying clients and the capacity to do the work, you'll always have a job. You can rest peacefully in the knowledge that you'll never be told to pack up your desk by the end of the day, which is something that many employees live in fear of.

Both men and women say that job loss is one of their biggest workplace fears,[20] and new mums arguably feel most vulnerable. A 2016 UK government report found that around one in nine mothers reported that they were either dismissed, made compulsorily redundant (where others in their workplace were not) or treated so poorly they felt they had to leave their job.[21]

The good news is that a freelance business can be reactive. When big companies need to adjust to market trends or new regulations, it can cost them millions in everything from new products to training costs. When you're a sole trader, you can react at lightning speed and essentially acclimatise your business in real time. You don't need to shift a factory full of stock, pay hundreds of employees every month or wait on board members to figure out a strategy and send it down the chain of command. You *are* the chain of command, and if you're a good businessperson then you have a good chance of success.

Most people don't do several jobs at once. As a freelancer, you will likely have multiple clients who you work with at the same time. At the time of writing, I've just lost two clients because they don't need my services anymore. But guess what? I've got seven other clients on my books, which means I'll barely even notice the financial impact of saying goodbye. If I'm honest, it's given me the capacity to look for more work at a higher rate. That makes me feel pretty secure.

BREAK THROUGH THE CAREER CEILING

There once was a time when company loyalty automatically led to promotion. You did your time and hung around long enough and eventually you would be rewarded with a corner

Want to be in charge of a business? Start your own.

office with your name on the door. If that all sounds a bit *Mad Men*, then that's because it is. I mean I've been watching the show in tandem with writing this book, so it's literally all I can think about right now, but it's also what the workplace used to look like back then, i.e. last *century*.

Promotions were earnt and had to be gifted to you. But what can you do when you're ignored in favour of an outside hire or, worse, your boss just doesn't want to move you from the role you're currently excelling in? Freelancing lets you control your own journey, especially when you feel you've outgrown your current job title. Want to be in charge of a business? Start your own. It's much quicker (and more fulfilling) than trying to clamber up the ladder and fight off the competition to snatch that CEO spot.

NO MORE COMMUTING

Arguably one of the sweetest victories of self-employment is the sheer absence of a commute, with two out of five people in traditional employment reporting that commuting is the worst part of their day.[22] For those who drive, traffic jams can eat into morning appointments, precious family time in the evening and increase stress levels. Public transport on the other hand requires less concentration (allowing us to read books or listen to podcasts), but that doesn't necessarily mean it's any more enjoyable. I know from personal experience that standing on an overcrowded train platform on a Monday morning can be enough to trigger a panic attack of the highest order. Standing upright, squished next to a stranger for 45 minutes and paying for the pleasure seems like an unfair exchange in my opinion. That doesn't even take into account the other horrors of commuting, such as journey delays, uncomfortable temperatures, anti-social behaviour from other passengers and sexual assaults that can so often occur.

With freelancing, there is no more running for the bus, no more scraping your car in the cold of winter and no more sitting in evening rush-hour traffic when you could be at home tucking into a pizza and watching reruns of *The Office*. I know what I'd rather be doing.

YOU CAN TRAVEL

Ah, the globetrotter. The freelancer who wants to work tirelessly for six months to raise enough funds to go backpacking through the mountains of Peru for two weeks over Christmas. Some freelancers truly live the digital nomad dream, consciously building their work life around their passion for travel. That might involve renting in Europe for six months and then uprooting to work from Thailand. Others might actively look for freelance projects based in another country to give them an excuse to temporarily relocate. I don't see the appeal myself, but having the opportunity to work from any location while on holiday is pretty unique and I can understand why those who like to travel turn to freelancing.

My less exciting version of this is having the freedom to travel home to Scotland for a long weekend, avoiding the stress and expense of travelling at peak times and getting to spend more than just a few hours with family and friends. When I worked as a full-time employee I had to use my yearly holiday allowance to carve out visiting times throughout the year – now I can simply pack up my laptop and work from my mum's house for as long as I want. Getting to see my parents every evening or pop down to the local with my mates is so much easier and less chaotic because I've simply relocated my work environment instead of squeezing everything into a few precious days of annual leave.

FLEXIBILITY FOR CHILDCARE

Most families need two incomes to make ends meet, so having one parent with a flexible schedule adds more money to the pot and also has the potential to keep childcare costs low. Most parents in this situation will tell you that this way of working isn't a perfect solution. This is especially true when school holidays roll around and the freelancing parent is expected to keep the kids entertained and squeeze in a few hours of client work at the same time. However, there are some plus points that parents have shared with me. For example, having the opportunity to pick up their kids from school instead of relying on grandparents or childminders. Of course it's worth remembering that having the flexibility to finish work for this often means catching up with tasks at other times like evenings and weekends. I've also heard of groups of freelance parents setting up a system where they each take it in turns watching all the kids to give the other freelancers time to focus. The majority of freelance parents still need to pay for some sort of childcare to allow them to get on with their work, but one of the best things about freelancing is that there is generally no daily commute involved. This means that transport delays are less of an issue and late pick-up fees can be avoided (some childcare providers will charge parents anywhere between £1 and £5 per minute when they arrive late to pick up their kids).

FLEXIBILITY FOR THOSE COPING WITH ILLNESS/DISABILITY

The more I've talked to people about why they've decided to go freelance, the more I've found that career changes often happen by accident. Take Sara Tasker for example. You wouldn't think that a bestselling author, podcaster and Instagram expert with over 200k followers would admit to 'falling into' the freelance life. But that's kind of what happened.

She started her Instagram account when she was on maternity leave, purely as a way to connect with others as a new mum. One thing led to another and within its first year her business – Me & Orla – turned over £35,000. She left her NHS job as a speech therapist because the 'pay was lousy and deep down I knew that I wasn't fulfilling my potential', but there was another big advantage to Sara deciding to work from home. She has a chronic illness called dysautonomia. Symptoms can include a rapid heart rate, severe fatigue, fainting when standing for too long and heat intolerance.

In a 2019 interview with the *Sun* newspaper, Sara said of her illness, 'It can be pretty disabling and there are days when I can barely leave the house. Sometimes I'll have to take the shower sitting down or I won't be able to take the stairs. The good thing is I managed to build my business around these limitations. I can run most of it from my phone or computer in bed.'

But setting up shop and going it alone hasn't meant taking a pay cut; she has since reported that her business turns over close to £250,000. Obviously not everyone is going to make such a sizeable income, but Sara has gained the flexibility she needs to take care of herself, and that has arguably had the biggest impact of all.

According to the Office for National Statistics the number of self-employed disabled people in the UK has risen by 30% since 2014. Disabled people account for 14% of the self-employed workforce – amounting to roughly 611,000 people[23] – and nearly half have been freelancing for a decade or more. In America, one out of five freelancers face health challenges that would prevent them from working if it weren't for freelancing.[24] Although there is need for further research, some studies conclude that traditional employment tends to be less accommodating for certain conditions and impairments. One survey also found that disabled people work in freelancing because of better work conditions, better job satisfaction as well as a desire to maintain or increase income.[25]

MENTAL HEALTH BENEFITS

One of the main reasons I wanted to be self-employed was to give myself permission to take mental health days. I've been living with depression and anxiety for eight years now and have seen varying levels of prejudice from employers in relation to mental health. Some of it was directed at me, some of it was said in my presence about others in a similar position, and some of it was not-so-subtly inferred. Most of the negative conversations around mental health were not specifically aimed at anyone, but derogatory and hard to hear nonetheless. I felt pressure to show up to work every day and pretend to be okay. It was a state of being that took a sh*t-tonne of energy that often I didn't have.

My personal foray into freelancing has therefore been heavily influenced by my mental illness. Rocking up to work with an anxiety disorder and depressive tendencies is – all jokes aside – a major inconvenience. I hope that one day mental illnesses will be accommodated in traditional workplaces, but until then, having control over my own workload and schedule has been a major positive in my life.

Although I like to talk openly about the mental health benefits of freelancing, I'm keen to bring a balanced view to the topic, and the figures certainly help with that.

In a 2019 survey conducted by Leapers, freelancers were asked the main reasons that they chose to work independently. The results found that 'improving mental health' was a motivator for just 29% of freelancers. Surprisingly, though, 56% of freelancers said that they think about their mental health more now than before they went self-employed. It's not necessarily the self-employment that brings relief (that itself comes with negative aspects which I'll cover in depth later in the book), but, instead, shedding the weight of a toxic work environment that feels so damn good.

Author Poorna Bell had this to say about her leap from the corporate world:

> With my role at HuffPost, I really loved the job I was doing but it was getting to that tipping point where had I continued to do the job I would have grown to resent it. It would have been too much stress to handle and when you manage a big team of people and you're

responsible for so many people that [stress] trickles down into their daily working lives as well and that was something I really didn't want to happen.

DESIGN YOUR OWN CAREER AND AVOID THE PIGEONHOLE

I don't think anyone has just one passion or skill. Even if you're obsessed with fashion, the chances are you're probably really good at something else creative, like photography or interior design. My older brother has always played drums in various bands throughout his life, but he's also done stints as a graphic designer and now he's really into abstract oil painting. He's currently learning to be a tattoo artist. At school, most of us were told to focus on one area and work really hard. No one likes a 'jack of all trades', or so it seemed. Realistically, however, very few of us are going to be completely satisfied doing one type of work for the rest of our lives.

The portfolio career is something that has seen somewhat of a re-brand in recent years, with Emma Gannon's book *The Multi-Hyphen Method: Work Less, Create More and Design a Career That Works For You* (Hodder & Stoughton, 2018) offering a manifesto of sorts for those of us who don't want to be pigeon-holed. I certainly found inspiration, and permission, to take the path less travelled after reading it. I've always aspired to have a job that reflects all the different facets of who I am, and a multi-hyphenate style of working makes this a reality. As Gannon acknowledges:

Sure, it makes the 'What do you do?' question harder to answer, but your identity becomes less about what your singular job title is. It becomes more about who you are, what you are interested in, what pays the bills and what your hobbies are. All these things make up your different 'hyphens'. You are a career chameleon, changing and moulding yourself to different projects.

Whereas chopping and changing industries used to be seen as evidence of a lack of direction, I'd argue that it's now seen as a willingness to follow your passions, even as they change over time.

I know one woman who built up her design portfolio doing branding and logos as a freelancer, which led to a full-time role with a company. She took on the job, gained valuable experience as an employee, and then used that to change plans yet again, setting up a product-based business selling her own prints, mugs and clothing items.

That's the great thing about freelancing: it doesn't have to be forever. That OOO feeling doesn't mean never having a boss ever again; it means living your own version of freedom, however it works for you, depending on your current needs and circumstances.

ON-THE-JOB EXPERIENCE

I needed writing experience in order to get paid work for publications, and that led me into freelancing. Instead of waiting around to see a vacancy for an internship or making plans to get a degree in journalism, I wrote on my blog and for as many other websites as I could, even if it was for free or paid very little. After a year of freelancing I could easily have used my experience as a stepping stone into a full-time role as a copywriter, if that's what I wanted to do (I didn't).

Of course, it's fine to go down the internship and/or degree route if that's what you decide, but if you can get hands-on experience in your industry by setting up your own freelancing business, then I say go for it, because no amount of training compares to actually doing the job yourself, day in, day out.

YOU MIGHT JUST GET TO MAKE A DIFFERENCE

You don't have to love your job. There are other things to get excited about in life, but there are some people who need to have a career that aligns with their personal values. Lots of us are bored at work or feel resentment because we bust a gut to line someone else's pockets. We see how decisions from management impact the whole team or feel like we have creative ideas that get blatantly ignored. Freelancing offers you a blank slate. The chance to make the most of your skills in an area that you're passionate about.

Maybe you're an HR expert and you specialise in creating a healthy work environment in your company and now you want to go into companies and train teams to do the same. Maybe you've become disillusioned as a wedding planner and want to run events for single women in your local area to foster a sense of community. Or maybe (and this is okay too) you're not quite sure what you want to do but you know it's going to be more meaningful than everything that went before.

Going freelance means you can address some of the issues that currently make your working life difficult. It's not a quick fix by any means, but it gives you the chance to tap into your passions and harness skills that might be under-utilised in your current role. It's hard work, but it has so many invaluable benefits, such as flexible hours, the opportunity to work in multiple industries, the freedom to embark on a wide spectrum of projects and the ability to step away from the mental pressures of a typical workplace. On top of all that, the sense of achievement that comes from freelancing really is magical. I still get stressed and over-worked, but it's all in the name of growing something that yields the most glorious results.

CURIOSITY

I'm going to hedge my bets and say that there are a sh*t tonne of you out there who identify with at least one of the reasons for going freelance that I've mentioned in this chapter. Personally, I got into freelancing for a few reasons. I hated the monotonous repetition of working in a café and I wanted the prospect of earning more than the minimum wage without having to go back into a management role. I had a feeling – a need – to see what I was capable of. Maybe all you have is an urge. A sense that you are destined for something different. It might not be a dream of changing the world, but simply a dream of changing *your* world. And that's enough.

Me, I was curious. And they say that's what killed the cat.

Well, I guess I was ready to be a dead cat.

TIP: Write a list of all the benefits you think freelancing will give you personally. Then write a list of benefits you get from your current job role and compare the two. Does freelancing still look like the best option?

CHAPTER 3

FACING FACTS

This is where it gets real. I want nothing more than for you to get that OOO feeling, but I'm not going to paint a perfect picture of what freelancing looks like. Get ready for a painfully realistic snapshot, like an unflattering portrait taken from down low when you unlock your phone without realising the camera is in selfie mode. Yup. This is going to be warts and all.

FREELANCING DREAM VS FREELANCING REALITY

Dream: You can work from anywhere. A beach. A treehouse. A cabin on the lake.

Reality: You will mostly work from a desk, sofa or kitchen table. If you get sick and you're on a deadline, you might even work from the toilet. Sometimes you'll need a change of scenery (or free WiFi and heating) and make the pilgrimage to a nearby café, where you begrudgingly pay a tenner for tea and a toastie.

Dream: You can pick and choose to work on the things you really love.

Reality: Every now and again you'll work with your dream client. You'll get to do something that pushes all your buttons, something that you're truly proud of. The rest of the time you'll be working on stuff that pays the bills and gives you the time to work on fun (badly paid) stuff.

Dream: You can work out whenever you like.

Reality: Getting dressed is optional. Leaving the house to go to the gym? Pah! Good luck.

Dream: You'll awake with the larks and take a morning stroll around the park before you start work.

Reality: You might manage a morning stroll to take the bins out but this is merely a procrastination technique.

Dream: You'll earn more money than if you were a company employee.

Reality: Once you put aside money for tax and expenses, you might be surprised at how little goes in your pocket. Oh, also, lots of people will expect you to work for free. Some of them will even be your friends.

You get the picture. Obviously, this is all a bit tongue in cheek, but the point I'm trying to make is that whichever Instagram version of freelancing you're hoping for (an inexplicably tidy Ikea desk featuring a ginormous Mac screen, or a pristine laptop nestled in a perfectly un-made bed, Starbucks cup slightly out of focus), this isn't real life. Just like any job, it comes with its bad days. Most freelancers

You might be making a mental list of reasons not to make the leap.

work alone, so you will probably find yourself doing tasks that you really don't want to do, like chasing invoices, having difficult conversations with a client, filing receipts or doing your taxes. These are the lesser-publicised aspects of freelancing which are likely to fall on you unless you hire outside help.

One of my favourite examples of why we should all learn to put up with the hard parts of any job comes from astronaut Peggy Whitson, who says that although peeing in space is a doddle, pooping is a pain in the ass. Explaining the process, USA Today[26] writes:

> the poop is sealed inside a plastic bag and hauled off the next space trash day… when it's too full, astronauts must 'put a rubber glove on and pack it down.' That's what happens when the ISS toilet is working. When it malfunctions, astronauts will occasionally have to deal with floating poop.

… Floating. Poop.

The most skilled and intelligent scientists on this earth (as of 17th June 2018, only 561 people have gone to space) are willing – dare I say, happy? – to deal with floating poop in order to do the job they love. Your tax return doesn't seem so daunting now, does it?

Now that I've taken your Insta-dreams of freelancing and crushed them to a pulp, I'm guessing you might be making a mental list of reasons not to make the leap. There are plenty of valid arguments for choosing regular employment over self-employment, I can't deny that. It's not for everyone.

But there comes a point where you may need to admit that your 'reasons' are just excuses or, even worse, they're just the opinions of other people that you've decided are truths. Let's take a look at some of the stumbling blocks that lie ahead and figure out fact from fiction, shall we?

CHAPTER 4

WHAT'S HOLDING YOU BACK?

There are SO many reasons not to go freelance. In the same way that there are so many reasons not take any type of risk. The list that follows includes, in my experience, the most common things that hold people back from taking a chance on their OOO dream. Some are genuine practical concerns that are worth worrying about; most, however, are rooted in self-doubt. The good news is that you can totally work towards shooing those away like a gang of hungry seagulls.

MONEY

Worrying about money is healthy. It's normal. Money won't buy you affection (The Beatles taught us that) but listen, lads, money does buy you electricity and warm water and a house to live in and bagels and peanut butter and an overpriced bath bomb that will ultimately fizzle away to nothing. Money isn't everything, but it absolutely should be a priority when you go freelance.

It would be entirely irresponsible of me to tell you to quit your job and go freelance if you're not 100% certain that you'll make enough money to make ends meet. There are some people who will tell you to hand in your notice and set up shop, claiming that a fire in your belly will force you to manifest a roster full of clients from thin air, just in time for when your rent is due. That might happen if you're lucky, but it's highly unlikely.

You need to think long and hard about how you're going to secure a regular income *before* you go freelance and even consider making it a side hustle (see box on p. 44) initially.

You don't necessarily need confidence to make money, but you do need clients, and having more clients will make you feel more confident in your abilities to pay your bills and live that OOO life for realsies.

With that in mind, I would suggest:

- Securing a base of clients to cover your basic costs before you make the leap
- Alleviating money worries by saving up enough to cover your outgoings for the first six months while you find ongoing work
- Working part-time to cover those outgoings instead
- Signing up to a temp agency to take ad-hoc shifts in an emergency
- Finding out whether there is an agency in your industry that will hand you clients for a fee

TIP: Make a list of all the ways you could earn money as a freelancer, even if you don't have the skills or the clients yet.

I don't make a lot of money as a freelancer and I still rely on my husband to help me out from time to time. I know that might shock some of you, but I know plenty of freelancers who work in cafés or office jobs a few days a week to subsidise their income. I have a strict food budget, I rarely have enough money for a visit to the hairdressers (hello, box dye) and I regularly visit discount stores. But that's just how I prefer to live. I could probably make more money doing something different like copywriting for an agency or running social media platforms for a big brand. But I do what I do because money isn't what makes me happy. I just need enough to pay for my basic outgoings and maybe a nice bottle of wine on a Friday night and I'm happy. You might have different expectations of life and obviously everyone's financial situation is completely unique, so be honest with yourself in terms of how much money you need to make in order to sustain a way of life that comfortably covers all your bills and makes you happy.

LACK OF TIME

If you're currently working a full-time job, enjoying a thriving social life, taking up hobbies on your days off and travelling the world whenever you get the chance, then you're probably thinking you have zero time to get into freelancing. Even reading a book like this can take weeks if you have a busy schedule to navigate. I get it. I'm not going to say you have the same number of hours in the day as Beyoncé (that's officially my most hated motivational quote of all time), but I am going to say that you can find more time if you really want to.

I'm willing to agree that you probably can't find an extra 10–15 hours every week to do market research, write a business plan and attend three networking events to schmooze with potential clients. But what's the rush? Just two hours a week adds up to 104 hours a year, which is better than no time at all. That could be the time you need to build an audience on social media, write a weekly blog post, start a podcast or brush up your skills on a certain piece of software. You could make the most of your holiday allowance by using a week to go on a training course or get stuck into some of the more time-consuming aspects of getting started. At the end of the week you could have a fully functioning website or a range of digital products ready to sell.

Once you've laid the foundations you can transition into starting a side hustle, which, again, doesn't necessarily need to take up a large chunk of your time. You can play the long game and build up your business at a pace that suits you.

WHAT IS A 'SIDE HUSTLE'?

The term 'side hustle' means something different to everyone. For some, it means a passion project that is never meant to become profitable; for others, it's a million-dollar idea that they work on tirelessly in order to turn it into a full-time job. When I talk about side hustles I generally refer to them as a smart way to dip your toe into freelancing without quitting your job entirely or setting up a fully-fledged business with an office and stock, etc. To me, side-hustling is a safe, slow-burn route to achieving a successful freelancing career.

LACK OF QUALIFICATIONS

One of the reasons you might have pressed pause on your freelancing dream is because you believe you don't have the necessary skills or formal qualifications. Often, however, this is just fear talking and not actually representative of your ability to get the job done. You probably do have the skills, but you're just afraid. Afraid of failing.

When I left school I decided to study music at university, but after the first year or so I realised that although I was enjoying the course, I had no real desire to get a job in the industry. However, I stuck it out and got my degree, even though I'm pretty sure I'd be turned away if I offered to do the coffee run at a record label, never mind actually hold some form of genuine responsibility.

Cut to over ten years later and here I am as an author, journalist and generally-will-write-for-money freelancer. I don't have a degree in English, creative writing or journalism, but I didn't let that stop me. I didn't get hired as a writer straight off the bat; I simply started practising. I wrote on my blog. I wrote an eBook. I wrote for other bloggers. I wrote for charity websites. I got one of my first paying gigs writing about video marketing – of all things – and I still have that client to this day. I had no formal training other than a few creative-writing classes that I did in the evenings after I graduated. But guess what? Sometimes you don't need training.

Amy Poehler, goddess full of feminine wisdom, puts it better than I ever could when she wrote in her book *Yes, Please:* 'You *do* it because the *doing* of it is the *thing*. The *doing* is the *thing*. The talking and worrying and thinking is not the *thing*.'

Amen, Amy.

Someone believed that the work I did was worth paying for and that helped me believe that I was good enough.

Sometimes, there's nothing to beat just doing the thing and seeing what happens. And I think that you know this is true, but you're using lack of training as an excuse to avoid doing the thing. Well, that just won't wash with me. Because unless you're an untrained dentist trying to pull over-grown molars out of someone's face, then I don't believe you.

TIP: Listen to podcast interviews from people in the industry you'd like to freelance in and take note of their journey. How did they build up their skill set?

LACK OF SELF-BELIEF

When I was twenty-six years old I had a mental breakdown, was diagnosed with depression, lived with suicidal thoughts and developed social anxiety during my recovery (it's all in my first book, *Depression in a Digital Age*, if you want the deets). I was on long-term sick leave from an intense management job, and I had an urge to do something creative.

So I found a side hustle, writing blog posts for a lifestyle website. I had no intention of being paid to do the work (thanks, disastrously low self-esteem) but eventually the woman running the website offered to pay me. After months of feeling lost and unfulfilled I finally saw a little glimmer of hope. Someone believed that the work I did was worth paying for and that helped me believe that I was good enough.

Self-belief is something that comes with practise and reassurance. Yes, you need to make the decision to get started as a freelancer and accept you'll make mistakes, but you also need to make the conscious effort to acknowledge all the small wins along the way.

Everyone has an inner critic living inside their heads. They are shaped by the kid who bullied them at primary school, the partner who said they were worthless or the boss who shamed them for thinking that baby kale was a small bird and not a vegetable. But that negative voice, that narrative that says you're not good enough, it's not fact. It's just a voice. And when you start to hear it and become more aware of its presence, you can respond with the facts. You are not a little kid anymore, and although you can't control past experiences, you CAN control the way you act in the future. You are good enough, and you deserve this.

TIP: Write a list of all the things you would do if you knew you couldn't fail. I bet some of them are totally doable!

IMPOSTER SYNDROME

Oh, Leo. I knew I'd find a way to subtly squeeze you into these pages.

When I was growing up in the 90s there was no one I loved more than Leonardo DiCaprio. I mean my parents were kind and provided me with food and shelter and what not, but Leo stole my heart. The reason I bring him up here, however, is totally unrelated to my teenage unrequited love.

I want to talk about a major stumbling block that many freelancers face before they take the plunge. In fact, it happens at every stage of running a business and can actually become more apparent as you become more successful. It's called 'imposter syndrome' and it's estimated that 70% of Americans[27] experience it at some point in their lives . The concept was first recognised in the late 70s by Pauline Rose Clance and Suzanne Imes, who said that it occurred less frequently and less intensely in men, making it a more likely problem for women. The syndrome is defined as a psychological pattern in which you doubt your accomplishments. It manifests itself as a persistent, internalised fear of being exposed as a fraud, even though the person is anything but. It's a fear of being 'found out'. It's now generally accepted that both men and women can succumb to feelings of imposterism, and social media platforms such as Instagram have been blamed for a resurgence in the issue for millennials. We're bombarded with powerful imagery that amplifies the achievements of others which can trigger feelings of comparison and inadequacy.

Maybe you have a degree in English but you feel unqualified to write for a living. Maybe you've won a blogging award but you never introduce yourself as a blogger. Maybe friends and family constantly ask you to create artwork and logos but you would never dare to advertise yourself as a designer. Maybe you're the self-appointed agony aunt in your circle, but don't feel confident enough to sign up for that life-coach training.

I like to use Leonardo DiCaprio in this context because he is well known for playing one of history's greatest imposters in the movie *Catch Me If You Can*. The film is based on the real-life story of Frank Abagnale, who became notorious after assuming multiple identities, including that of an airline pilot, lawyer, doctor and US Bureau of Prisons agent. He was the ultimate conman and (spoiler alert!) was eventually caught after a spree that took place between the ages of fifteen and twenty-one.

So, if you think you're an imposter, I'm sorry, but you're wrong. You have nothing to be worried about. The real imposters are sneaky, deluded and willing to do whatever it takes to assume a persona that will get them what they want. They're not sitting at home wondering whether they have the right to put the word 'blogger' on their LinkedIn profile page. You're not an imposter. You're just learning to grow into the identity that you already own.

Overcoming imposter syndrome is something that gets easier once you start controlling your own narrative. You need to start walking and talking like you know what you're doing. You need to feign confidence in order to instil it in yourself. A great place to start is online. Spend a few hours revamping your social media platforms to include the thing that you want to freelance in. It could be writing, pottery making, illustrating, teaching yoga or the guitar. Whatever it is, you need to start believing that you ARE that person who is DOING the thing. Rewrite your social media bios to include your freelancing dream, and do it fearlessly. Don't call yourself a budding writer. You *are* a writer! The more you drip-feed these positive messages into your online persona, the more comfortable you'll become with believing them in real life.

TIP: Make some basic business cards that you can use when you go freelance. You don't have to show them to anyone just yet; just try them on for size and wear them around the house for a few weeks. Then, when you're ready, you can take a walk in your new threads.

FEAR OF COMPETITION

Okay, let's be real for a second. You're amazing. You're capable. You're a flippin' freelance god or goddess in the making. But you're not the only one.

Freelancing is becoming an attractive prospect for a lot of people nowadays, especially women (IPSE reports a 63% increase since 2008 in the UK alone[28]), so you may find yourself competing for work. It used to be that writers had to show up in a bustling city centre office to meet with editors, to use the telephones and of course type up stories on typewriters. Now they work remotely, chasing stories and writing them up on smartphones or laptops. Sales people used to stand in stores and wait for customers to appear; now they're at home building email marketing campaigns and sales funnels to entice people into purchasing. Even delivery drivers now use their own vehicles instead of a company van. There are hundreds and thousands of freelance roles that simply did not exist ten years ago, and companies are starting to see that this is a smart way to hire.

I bet that you know at least two or three people who have done or still do freelance work in some capacity, and that number will only grow. So be aware that when you jump into that big pool of freelancers, you might start to feel inadequate. It's only natural to compare yourself to others, especially when you're just starting out. But please don't use this comparison as an excuse not to get started. In my early days as a blogger, had I compared my success to that of Tanya Burr or Zoe Sugg, I would've felt like absolute sh*t. They were racking up millions of followers, getting brand sponsorship and designing their own bloody beauty advent calendars, and there I was, writing two or three blog posts a week and popping a bottle of Aldi prosecco if I got over twenty page views in a week. Comparison wouldn't have served me well back then, and it still doesn't today.

Instead of looking at what other freelancers have achieved and seeing it as competition, try to see it as motivation: living proof that there is work out there to be done and opportunities to be grasped. Yes, some people you idolise will have better qualifications, more money, industry connections and years of experience. But maybe they aren't really the people you should be idolising. Find the people who worked hard, played the long game and took chances. Those people are evidence that with determination you can break into freelancing and be successful.

I remember the exact moment I felt comparison work its magic on me. It was the day that a new hardback book arrived in the post with the name Estee Lalonde written on the front. Estee is a Canadian YouTube star who has been living in London since her early twenties, making videos about beauty, fashion and her lovable greyhound Reggie (who sadly passed away when I was writing this book). I'd been following her since the early days (total fangirl) and didn't think twice about preordering her book, *Bloom*, when it was released in 2016. As I flicked through the pages of her memoir-cum-self-help-book on the day it fell through my letterbox, it could have been easy to feel jealousy towards the blue-eyed, blonde-haired girl who had gone from being a complete stranger in London to basically owning the influencer scene, with global brands falling over themselves to work with her. Instead, I saw her evolution from bedroom blogger to bestselling author as the evidence I needed to see that anything is possible. Instead of questioning what right I had to create something of my own, instead of asking, 'Why me?', I thought with a quiet confidence, 'Why *not* me?'

Hopefully throughout this chapter you've started to question the internal dialogue that could potentially limit you from embarking on your career as a freelancer. I get that it's a scary prospect to move into a whole new world where there seems to be so much uncertainty, so much that could potentially go wrong. In the next chapter I'll lift the lid on some of these pain points to give you an honest idea of what you expect from your OOO future.

CHAPTER 5

WHAT YOU SHOULD KNOW BEFORE TAKING THE LEAP

Everyone talks about leaps of faith. You know, that pivotal scene in every coming-of-age movie where the scrappy lil' teenager has to jump over the metaphorical river to become the hero? All his friends are on the other side saying, 'Do it! Just jump!' Well, that's all very encouraging, but if *you* were about to jump, wouldn't you do a few routine checks first? You know, make sure your shoelaces are tied, pick a nice big rock to potentially land on, and check there isn't a gang of hungry alligators plotting your demise from further down the river? I know I would.

With that in mind, here are some things I want you to consider while you limber up for your Oscar-worthy leap into freelancing.

WHO YOU ARE

Woaaah! We're only on Chapter 5 and already throwing out the existential questions! Don't worry, we're not digging too deep just yet, but if you want to live the OOO life you need to be closely in tune with yourself. From your personality type to your preferred working style, these nuggets of knowledge will serve you well as you become your own boss. Even seemingly irrelevant information such as what time of the day you get most hangry will help you lead a more fulfilled and successful working life.

There are lots of different personality types as well as methods and frameworks for learning to make the most of your natural working style. The book *Work Simply: Embracing The Power of Your Personal Productivity Style* by Carson Tate is an excellent place to start, as it drills down into four common working styles. (Go to Chapter 18 to read more about how to identify your working style and how to maximise your productivity.)

The most famous personality types are the infamous A and B. Type A personalities are known to be competitive high achievers, time-urgent, conscientious and sometimes hostile and aggressive. Type B personalities are generally more patient, relaxed, easy-going and have a tendency to procrastinate. They are also more likely to explore possibilities and 'play things by ear'. If the thought of living your life like either of these stresses you out, then you've probably figured out exactly which personality type you are. (Hint: it's the other one.) However, each type does exist on a continuum, so it's not an exact science.

I think I sway towards Type A, although I'm not a textbook example. I am highly sensitive, fly off the handle easily and try to cram too much into my day. I often over-schedule myself and use productivity as a measure for happiness without actually taking much satisfaction from being productive. I'm impatient and have an unrealistic notion that multitasking is effective. I've painted a somewhat dreary picture of myself, partly because it's funny and partly because it's true, but honestly, there are plenty of aspects of my personality that might seem negative in the first instance but actually lend themselves well to the freelance lifestyle. For example, impatience got my first book submitted to the publisher two weeks ahead of schedule. My highly sensitive nature has made me self-reflective about how I receive criticism from magazine editors and helps me improve my pitching skills. My obsession with multi-tasking means I have listened to the entire back catalogue of my favourite true crime podcasts while getting in a daily walk around the local nature reserve.

Type B personalities are like my dad. They take enjoyment from things without being competitive. They run for the love of running without checking their Fitbit to see how many miles they've covered. They tolerate most people without a fuss and enjoy creative things like art and music. Do these behaviours mean that my dad makes a terrible freelancer? Absolutely not. He's been self-employed for over twenty years and has always been busy. He gets repeat business because he's friendly and easy to work with. He works long hours but it doesn't make him agitated or anxious. I've never seen him multi-task. He just systematically gets sh*t done.

Some people argue that a certain personality type will get you further ahead than another. F*ck that. For years, extroverts were hailed as having the optimum traits for effective management, with the confidence and charm needed to control a room. Now, however, it's the introverts who are fast becoming the calm and collected leaders the world needs.

In her book *Quiet: The Power of Introverts in a World That Can't Stop Talking* (Penguin, 2012), Susan Cain discusses the idea that modern Western society celebrates and rewards extroverts by default. She writes about students at Harvard who feel pressured to be loud and sociable in order to succeed, and holds up real proof that extroverts are more likely to be employed or promoted even if there are more qualified introverts in the running. Nevertheless, there's an argument that introvert tendencies can be just as effective as their extrovert counterparts, and both personality types are key to a successful business. As Cain writes:

> *Introverts and extroverts also direct their attention differently: if you leave them to their own devices, the introverts tend to sit around wondering about things, imagining things, recalling events from their past, and making plans for the future. The extroverts are more likely to focus on what's happening around them. It's as if extroverts are seeing 'what is' while their introverted peers are asking 'what if.'*

Whatever your personality type, there is a place in the world of work for you, and freelancing might just be the vehicle to transport you to unprecedented job satisfaction. But knowing yourself is key to keeping the engine running and avoiding breakdown.

TIP: Read *Work Simply: Embracing the Power of Your Personal Productivity Style* by Carson Tate. It will help you identify your preferred style of working and offers lots of insights into how you can manage tasks appropriately. I found a copy in my local library 'cause I'm cool like that.

SELF-MOTIVATION IS KEY

Whatever your personality type, freelancing is going to require you to be a good leader. Thought being a team of one would get you out of boardroom duties? Think again. There is only one person who can set the tone for your business and it's you. If you want to be your own boss, then you're going to have to do just that. Be the boss.

Motivating yourself to get sh*t done is quite easy in the beginning, especially if you're working on a side hustle before you make the leap. I was working in a boring catering job while I blogged in the evenings and the reality of making coffees and frying bacon for a living really motivated me to work hard on my own business. I'm not saying that working in a café is bad, but for me it just wasn't creatively satisfying and that left a gaping hole inside of me that I so desperately wanted to fill. I was motivated to take opportunities that other people may not have taken (like unpaid writing gigs) because I wanted to explore any avenue that could potentially give me a way out of my day job. When I started to see paid gigs coming through, that gave me an even bigger boost. Just £20 here and there reminded me that I was slowly getting somewhere, and that I was moving in the right direction.

Now that I'm fully freelance, the motivation is often quite primal. It's survival. I'd love to say that I'm creatively driven by all the projects I work on, but that's not realistic. I work on a lot of basic jobs that can be a little bit boring, but they pay the bills and they don't involve bacon butties. In between the motivation to pay my bills, I work towards long-term goals which are more creatively fulfilling. It's like dangling a carrot to tempt a bunny in the right direction. Big, fun projects like writing this book take up a lot of time and don't pay a great deal, but I know that getting up early to work on the boring jobs is essential to afford me the time to do the aspects of my job that I really enjoy. Like writing about dangly carrots.

There are lots of other ways to trick yourself into feeling motivated that I'll explain later in the book, but, for now, consider your personality type and think about how you'll get yourself out of bed in the morning without the fear of being reprimanded by a superior. How will you meet deadlines and chase new work in a few months or even a few years from now? Will you manage to stop yourself from being a Type A workaholic? Are you likely to hide away from challenges (like public speaking or networking) that could potentially lead to more work? Will you be able to create a daily routine that serves your business, or does routine scare you? All these questions should be thought about before you make the leap into self-employment.

TIME IS OUR CURRENCY (TAKE THAT TO THE BANK)

Freelancing is seen as a luxury to some, a lifestyle choice based on a notion that we are free to do what we want. And yes, we are free in some respects, but in others we are chained down by what people expect of us. We have flexibility that other people want to abuse, but we need to remember that, for us, time is our livelihood. Time spent on other things eats into time we could be spending building the business or doing paid work. Protecting your time is essentially as important as having a cryptic password for your online banking. You

You wouldn't let anyone steal your earnings, so don't let anyone rob you of your time.

wouldn't let anyone steal your earnings, so don't let anyone rob you of your time. You can choose to give it to others of course, but make sure that it's your decision and one that you're comfortable with.

Of course, sometimes it's really us who is stealing time. I'm the first to admit that I often spend a little too long checking Instagram when I should be writing. I decide to make an elaborate vegan brunch at 11 am when I have a mountain of paperwork to attend to. The urge to procrastinate when you're a freelancer is intense, and the repercussions aren't as immediate as they might be if you worked in an office with a boss breathing down your neck. There's no one to cast a judgemental glance when you start late for the third morning in a row, or to remind you that rearranging your gallery wall in the spare bedroom isn't a priority right now. I'm all for a wee extended lunch break to watch a few episodes of *Fleabag*, but if you start to let that turn into the full season(s), then you're taking the p*ss. You don't need to be constantly working, but you also need to be realistic and understand that when you're not working, you're not earning a wage. And no one's going to come and pay your rent while you lie horizontal and ignore all your deadlines.

NON-FREELANCERS WON'T ALWAYS 'GET IT'

The one aspect of freelancing that I was not prepared for was the impact that it's had on my personal life. More specifically, my relationships. Overall it's made me feel more in control of my life – which I love – but I didn't know that it would alter what other people see when they look at me. People's expectations of me have changed.

As I've already explained, one of the main reasons I decided to go freelance was for the sake of my mental health. I wanted the ability to ride out bad days at home, in private, without having to explain to others why I didn't do any work that day or why I would be making up the hours at the weekend. I wanted the option to stay in bed and work there if that's how I felt, and I wanted to be able to sob as and when required without needing to hide in the bathroom to cover my shame. The freelance life delivered, mostly.

I do have the privilege of taking sick days if I want, although it's more like a sick morning or afternoon, followed by a longer work day to make up for the loss of earnings. I can be flexible with my time if I choose to be, but what some friends and family don't understand is that this is a decision for *me*. Not them.

When you work OOO, you tend to become the errand boy. The person who lets the boiler repair person in or takes in Amazon packages for the neighbours. Popping out to do a favour for someone might seem like a simple enough task, but what happens when a last-minute piece of work comes in or you have to get on a Skype call with a client? Mothers working from home are expected to step in as childminder during holidays or on sick days, even though their business still needs attention in their absence. When my husband is home sick, my entire day is thrown off as my space, which acts as 'office' during the day, is suddenly transformed into hospital ward, with old tissues and lozenge packets strewn across the floor while a Marvel film plays in the background. When visitors pop by for a coffee, how do I tell them I've got work to be getting on with when I have no office to be 'getting back to'? When everyone goes around the circle saying, 'How're things at work?', why am I repeatedly left out of the conversation?

Non-freelancers aren't the only fly in the ointment. There are plenty of people who will have something to say about your desire to sidestep the status quo, but that's not necessarily a bad thing. Depending on the kind of day I've had, you might even catch me, the enthusiastic freelancer, telling a newbie to run for the hills and get a 'proper' job. There is no one definitive answer to whether freelancing is good or bad. But there are a lot of loud voices out there when you start telling people you want to make the leap, so be prepared to deal with the noise.

CHAPTER 6

PEOPLE WILL TRY TO PUT YOU OFF

Be careful who you ask for advice about making the leap.

People will generally speak from their own experience and as a result, will have a positive or negative bias towards self-employment as a whole. If you seek advice from your uncle who set up his own business and went bankrupt, he'll probably tell you to steer clear. Your friend who's had a stable council job for fifteen years with regular promotions and a generous benefits package probably thinks you're mad for even considering giving up your salary.

Similarly, though, if you live in a social media bubble and surround yourself with entrepreneurs who say they make a six-figure income and work a mere two hours per day, you might get the wrong idea.

Everyone has an opinion on freelancing and it's up to you to figure out if it's right for *you*. You should definitely discuss the decision with friends and family, but be prepared for them to say one or all of the following:

'IT'S TOO RISKY'

In the beginning, yes, it's pretty risky to go freelance, and so you probably shouldn't make the leap until you've got some savings in the bank and a few regular clients on your books. If you went freelance without any skills, experience or means of income, then, yep, that's pretty f*cking risky.

But an established freelancer? Well, they've got several clients, and are potentially working on multiple projects at once. Because they work on an hourly or day rate (see page 136), they are more affordable for businesses who only need workers for a short period of time. They aren't pigeon-holed by job title and can normally accept a range of jobs that match up with their wide range of skills.

For example, I can run your social media accounts, edit your podcast and write blog posts. I can also pitch stories to magazines and get you some PR and write newsletters and product descriptions. So if suddenly no one is making podcasts or using social media anymore, I can turn to copywriting to make up for the lack of income. I have my fingers in many, many pies and there will always be scope to pivot as and when required.

If you work in a company role and all of a sudden everything goes tits up (in the way that the construction industry was destroyed by the 2008 recession), then sorry, but you're f*cked. Having different strands of income that you can pull on as circumstances change makes freelancing a dream for stability. You just have to work hard in the beginning to build up your skills and your client base to see the long-term benefits.

'YOU NEED TO HIRE A TEAM'

The beauty of being freelance is that you can dictate how your business is run. If you don't want the stress of managing employees and having enough money to pay their wages, then you don't need to. You can outsource work to other freelancers on a project-by-project basis and then go back to being a company of one as soon as the work is done or things quieten down.

Success doesn't depend on expansion. You can create a manageable, steady flow of work (and income) based on your own abilities if you find the right clients and price yourself appropriately. A team of one is arguably more sustainable as there are less overheads involved. If you thrive as an independent worker, then lean into that. I personally love nothing more than sitting at home in my pants while having a personal development meeting with, well, myself. I always get good feedback in those meetings.

'YOU NEED A BUSINESS PLAN'

Err, no. If you're going to the bank for a loan then sure, they'll probably want to see a business plan, but lots of online lenders don't ask for one. I wouldn't even recommend thinking about taking out a loan to start a business unless it's absolutely necessary (say you literally need a particular piece of kit or software to do the job), and even then I think it's more sensible to be patient and save up a pot of cash while working a regular job.

A business plan is a nice idea, but I think too many people think that it guarantees the success of your business. It doesn't. If I had written a business plan when I first went freelance, I would never have planned to do much of the work that pays my bills nowadays. I had a plan of sorts, but not an official strategy document based on market research and financial forecasts.

Being reactive is just as important as being proactive, because it means when opportunities pop up you're flexible and open to changing your trajectory. I started off trying to make money through sponsored content on my blog, but after a few months I was encouraged to pitch feature ideas to an online newspaper. Getting into journalism wasn't part of my 'plan', but when it cropped up as a potential earner, I gave it a bash. I wasn't restricted by a framework that I'd created to make me feel like I had my sh*t together. In fact, my sh*t was all over the shop, and as a result I ended up fulfilling a lifelong dream of mine by writing for major publications and getting two book deals.

'YOU'LL NEVER MAKE IT'

If you have an inkling of a feeling about setting up your own business, it can take years to simply convince yourself that you've got what it takes. Or, more accurately, that you've even got the right to dream big. Because many of us take such a beating from life in the form of abusive partners, pessimistic frenemies and over-protective parents, we think we are rubbish humans who must settle for Just A Job. There is nothing wrong with having Just A Job if that's what really makes you happy.

I had Just A Job back in 2013 when I was recovering from a mental breakdown. There are times to be passionate about your career goals and there are times to simply bring home the bacon. I had been off sick with depression for almost a year, regularly unable to face daily tasks such as showering or popping to the corner shop. So the thought of going back to the job I'd had previously – running a business, managing a

I really believe that if you've got the drive, you too can, in your own way, do the thing you want to do.

team, dealing with budgets and staff training – was too much to handle. I had to go back to basics if I wanted to return to the world of work, so that's what I did. I worked a part-time job as a waitress in a family-run café and it had no prospects. No likelihood of a pay rise or promotion. Was I hopping out of bed every morning, excited to serve lattes and toasted teacakes to local OAPs? No, but it was what I needed at the time: a simple vocation to build my confidence up.

Lots of other people have Just A Job because it funds other passions in life, like paddle boarding, knitting pyjamas for goats or bowling three times a week. That's fine. It's more than fine – it's excellent. But if you're working Just A Job and it's sucking your soul and you're wondering if there's a chance that you could be happy at work, don't let the negative voices (internal or external) tell you that work is supposed to make you miserable. We all have bad days. But I refuse to believe that anyone should accept unhappiness at work as the norm. It sounds really dramatic to say this, but you only have one life. Do you want to spend it doing something that you've settled for? Or do you want to look back and know that at the very least you gave this freelancing thing a bash?

SO, WHAT NOW?

That's my spiel. I, for the foreseeable future, have chosen to freelance for a living, and although it's not perfect, it's doable. And I think it's pretty f*cking cool. I really believe that if you've got the drive, you too can, in your own way, do the thing you want to do. It might be (definitely will be) hard work and you'll probably (100%) fail at some point. It might not make you much money and it might not be your full-time job. But don't let the fear of not being good enough hold you back. I think everyone deserves a chance to experience what that OOO life feels like, because, why the hell not?

THINGS TO REMEMBER

- Everyone is freelancing, especially women
- Companies are starting to address flexible working
- It's not as risky as you think and offers long-term benefits such as experience and the chance to pivot your career trajectory
- You won't necessarily be financially better off
- But it can come with increased job satisfaction and the opportunity to make a difference
- Self-belief and self-reflection are a **must** before you make the leap
- Your ability to self-motivate will be tested
- Friends and family might not get it, and they might even expect you to fail
- You'll probably never feel 'ready' to go freelance, but that's okay

PART TWO

RUNNING THE SHOW

CHAPTER 7

DON'T LET THE DOOR HIT YOU ON THE WAY OUT

So, you've flicked through my motivational – arguably off-putting – account of what to expect from freelancing. And you want it. You want it bad. You can taste sweet freedom in the air and you're pumped. You want the OOO life and you want it NOW. But hold your horses for just one minute…

How are you going to make this work?

There are lots of things to consider before you start drafting your resignation letter and hitting up Urban Outfitters for inspirational art prints to hang above your new desk. Here are the most important, in my humble opinion…

GET FINANCIALLY PREPARED

Quite simply, can you afford to go freelance? Start-up costs vary widely depending on the tools you'll need to get sh*t done as well as what you already have at your disposal. All I needed to get started as a writer was a laptop and an internet connection. Technically, I could've blogged directly from my phone, but it wouldn't have been easy, and we had a clunky laptop sitting at home that was much more efficient even though it wasn't top of the range.

What you'll need to get started is entirely up to you and will be different depending on the industry you plan to work in, but my advice would be to start small, with the plan to invest any profits back into the business to gradually get everything you need to grow and flourish. As I write this I'm several years into my career as a freelance writer and my business outgoings are about £200–£400 per month depending on what I have in my calendar. I've made decisions along the way to pay for services that make life easier, such as software and plugins. I've opted to make train journeys to speak at events or meet clients in real life instead of over the phone. I've bought online courses and ridiculously overpriced (but, I must protest, genuinely life-changing) stationery. In the beginning you may not need any of that.

Figure out the bare bones of what you need to get going, and then? GET GOING. Score a student discount off a mate for that editing software you need. Buy a refurbished camera to start taking photographs. Do a skill swap with a friend to get your initial website up and running. Work a few extra shifts to buy some stock for your online shop. Go slow and you'll grow.

TIP: Go through your bank statements and direct debits and make a realistic list of all your outgoings, including grocery shopping, basic socialising and a bit extra for birthdays and clothing. Can you minimise any expenses (unnecessary subscriptions, unused gym memberships, extravagant meals out) in order to set up a savings fund for your business? Could you still cover your outgoings if you went part-time in order to give yourself more time to get started with freelancing?

WORK THAT SIDE HUSTLE

I strongly advise that you do all of this while maintaining a steady income from another source. Even if you get a few well-paying jobs in the beginning, these aren't a basis for future income. It can be tempting to look at your first few freelance jobs and assume that your business will grow exponentially based on these figures, but you can't pick your best month in business and then multiply it by twelve to create an accurate yearly projection. The big project you're in talks about might never come to fruition. The client who hands you tonnes of work every month might change direction. The editor who commissions all your features might leave the newspaper. Things will dry up. It will more than likely rain again, but those dry spells WILL COME. So you need to make sure that you can support yourself when your business isn't making much money.

The simplest way to do this is to go freelance while working as a part-time or full-time employee. In fact, one in four Brits run a side hustle alongside a regular job.[29] Author and podcaster Emma Gannon explained that while researching the topic she found that almost everyone has some sort of side hustle idea that they are thinking about exploring.[30] From a chef who'd like to podcast to a pilot who is also a cinematographer, there's no limit to what you can achieve outside of the 9-to-5.

> TIP: Every employment agreement is unique, and yours might explicitly state that you are prevented from doing certain things such as working for a competitor, doing a job that could reflect badly on your employer or breaching the Working Time Regulations. You might need written permission to work freelance, so look closely at your terms of employment before you take that next step.

CONSIDER A PHASED EXIT

There are two ways to be a freelancer as an employee. You can do the freelancing in secret (but check your contract, because you might be legally obliged to tell your employer; see TIP above) or you can be an open book. Whichever route you pick is up to you. If your boss is a total jackass then it might be worth keeping quiet. I've met a few employers who take personal offence when their staff even hint at moving on, or even have priorities outside the business. Ask yourself:

- If you work in a toxic work environment, are your colleagues going to hold your new ambitions against you?
- Will they feel threatened and act out?
- Will talking about your freelance life inspire others, or will it simply make them feel angry about the fact that they are stuck grinding away in a stale workplace?

Only you know what's best for your current situation, and if you're not 100% certain then it's probably best to keep schtum until it feels right. You and your OOO dream might simply be too bootylicious for your colleagues to handle, and in the words of Destiny's Child, you must consider if they are indeed ready for this jelly.

If you feel like talking openly about your side project is an option, then that will make this next part easier.

Once you feel financially able (e.g. you've squirrelled away some savings or you have regular paid work on your books), you might want to consider asking to work less at your 9-to-5 job. If that sounds as scary as a bar that serves wine by the colour and not the country, then it's probably because it is. Working on a project on your days off is one thing, but actively choosing to let it impact the hours you work is another. Not only does it let your employees know that you're serious about this career pivot, it also means admitting to yourself that you're really committed to making it a success.

But the reality is that asking for reduced or more flexible hours at work can be a really effective way of easing into freelancing for those who want to take as little risk as possible – i.e. taking the leap while still having the safety net of a monthly pay check. If you choose to reduce your hours then, obviously, *duh*, your pay check will be affected. So bear this in mind if that's the route you choose. If your employer is up for it, you could try to rearrange your working week so that you do longer hours but over fewer days. This means you won't lose any income but you'll gain a day to focus on your new project. The other upside of course is that if your freelancing gig is going well, you could end up earning more in the long run as the jobs start rolling in.

This whole plan is kind of like a phased exit. You take a slow
and measured approach to quietly stepping away from your
employer. Sadly, this means there's unlikely to be a giant
'f*ck this' moment where you sprawl both arms across your
desk and swipe your paperwork, mug, stapler and a tiny fake
cactus onto the floor in a fit of rage. Instead, you'll taper
your hours down to part-time and eventually work your full
notice period, choosing to leave gracefully with a card and
some Zara gift vouchers from your colleagues.

HOW TO ASK YOUR EMPLOYER FOR FLEXIBLE WORKING HOURS

First of all, take a look at your contract of employment and
your employee handbook (go on, dig it out; you'll have
it somewhere) and find out if your company already has
any information on this. If you're lucky, they'll already have
guidelines in place about how to apply.

Depending on the laws in place in your country, you
may have a legal right to ask for flexible working hours.
Check your government website for more details.

I'll be honest and say up front that I have never made a written request for flexible working, probably because I've always worked for small businesses where contracts were clumsily written as an afterthought by employers who were preoccupied with an emergency dash to Costco or, more likely, secretly vaping in the back office. With my last and final employer there was simply no need for me to type up a letter, because we had a good working relationship. I just decided on what I thought were reasonable adjustments to my shift pattern and asked to speak to him privately to ask if this was possible. He said yes and this meant I only worked four days a week while I was taking in freelance writing work the rest of the time. When I went back a few months later and asked to lose yet another day to cope with the constant influx of work, he said no. Which was fair enough. It didn't suit the business and I think he could tell that I was beginning to prioritise my freelance work and that my days there were numbered. I handed in my notice a month later.

Self-worth coach Kat Nicholls asked for flexible working with her employer too. Here are her words on the subject:

I was working on my blog and training to be a coach outside of my Monday-to-Friday job and was getting to a point where I was burning out. I had two choices, I could either put the brakes on my blog and coaching work or I could approach the company I work for and reduce my hours there. I've been working at Memiah for over five years now and they are incredibly supportive of their

Getting ready to leave your job and go freelance is a buzz.

employees' out-of-work passions. They knew what I was doing with my blog and coaching work, and were more than happy to let me reduce my hours to fuel this. I also stepped back from my role as a manager. As much as I loved managing my team, it took up a lot of energy and headspace. Being able to hand the reins over to a team member who was ready for a new challenge allowed me to focus on writing and staff wellbeing.

I asked if she had any tips on how to ask for flexible working hours and she said:

If you need to speak to your employer, consider what benefits they will see from you working reduced hours. In my case, reducing my hours and stepping back from management has made me happier at work, less stressed and therefore more productive. I would say I'm performing better now than I was at five days a week, because I prioritised my mental health.

DON'T BURN BRIDGES

Getting ready to leave your job and go freelance is a buzz. It feels terrifying and exciting at the same time, like opting for the special blend at Starbucks or trying out blue mascara as a teenager (both these decisions ended badly for me, but I stand by the sentiment that they were risks worth taking, goddamnit). But remember that just because you're leaving now doesn't mean that you're better than anyone else. Don't pity those left behind, and do not leave on bad terms. You never know when you'll need to hit up a previous boss for a reference or some old pay slips. You also never know when you might need to go back looking for a job. In some cases a past employer might even be a future client.

AND REMEMBER: THERE IS NO SUCH THING AS A PERFECT START

When I was looking for a new diary a few months before I was a full-time freelancer, the task consumed me. Every time we walked into John Lewis I could almost hear my husband's eyes roll back in his head. *Here we go again. The quest for the perfect diary…*

I would spend thirty or forty minutes picking up every hardback, softback, monogrammable diary in the store. Making *mmmm* sounds, muttering phrases like 'it's not The One' under my breath and periodically gasping when I found something that I hadn't seen before. I would always walk away empty-handed, regularly wandering off into Paperchase or maybe even the Poundshop in the hopes that I would unearth a shiny gem to cater for all my organisational needs. I'm not saying that stationery isn't important (I have strong views on paper quality, margin placements and whether a diary week starts on a Sunday or a Monday), but there was no need for me to spend weeks sourcing a diary. What I was doing, in fact, was using the quest for the perfect diary as a reason not to have a diary. A distraction. How could I face my goals and put a plan into action if I didn't have anywhere to write it all down? I was waiting for the perfect thing to come along and make the time seem right, but it didn't exist.

There is no perfect diary. No matter which one you settle for there will always be others out there with fancier paper, extra stickers or bigger pages. Don't wait around for the time to be perfect, don't wait to feel 'ready', because you'll probably *never* feel ready. This doesn't mean that you shouldn't prepare, plan and work hard, but it does mean that you might need to muster up some self-belief to go out there and make it happen. You'll make a lot of mistakes no matter when you make the leap, so get used to saying sorry and learning from all the messes you've created.

As Marie Forleo wisely put it, 'The key to success is to start before you are ready.'

CHECKLIST

- Look at your finances
- Get some savings behind you
- Consider the side hustle approach
- Look into flexible working
- Leave on good terms
- Get comfortable with not feeling ready

CHAPTER 8

SETTING UP

Once you've got your finances in order, there are a few other things that you'll want to have in place before you go freelance, and I'll be going over these in this chapter. Some of them are essential, like registering as self-employed, and some are totally optional, like setting up a website or finding a nice co-working space.

I'm not going to act like I had all of these things fully in place before I went freelance because, as we now know (see page 84), there's no such thing as a perfect start. But if you check as many of these off your list from the get-go, you'll find your business runs a lot smoother as a result. It also means that when an insane amount of clients start clambering to work with you (trust me, it's going to happen), you're not messing about with the basic set-up when you could be getting stuck into the real work.

YOUR VIRTUAL SHOP FRONT

You can network and tweet people all you like, but when people are ready to make contact or hand over their money, they want to visit your website first. There's nothing more frustrating than talking to someone you would love to work with and then, when you go to find out more about their services, you discover that there's not a single trace of them on the internet other than their personal Facebook page.

The good news is that making a website can be as simple or as complicated as you like. Guess which end of the sliding scale I'm going to recommend you sway towards? Yep, you got it: make it simple AF.

When I started out I used a free blogging platform called WordPress, which is the most popular website builder in the world. I didn't know this at the time. I just picked the first one that popped up on a Google search. I chose a name, a colour scheme and a pre-made template and that was that. I was up and running in less than an hour. I'd put off doing it for weeks and when it was done I was surprised at how quick and easy it had been. Other free services that allow you to set up a basic website for free include Wix, Weebly and SITE123, although bear in mind that there will be an extra fee to purchase your domain name and this needs to be renewed yearly. There are also paid platforms such as Squarespace and GoDaddy.

TIP: If you're selling products online, you should consider setting up a website using Shopify. Experts say it's the best ecommerce website builder and is an industry leader in that respect.

REGISTERING AS SELF-EMPLOYED

If you're making money by selling goods or services
for a profit then you'll usually need to register with the
government as self-employed. Here in the UK it can be done
online[31] and really takes no time at all, so don't put if off for
any longer than you need to. If you're based outside the UK,
check your country's government website to find out more
information about how you can register as self-employed.

INSURANCE

The great thing about freelancing is that it's easy to get
into, but a lot of people are underprepared for the risks
and responsibilities that come with running a business. I
know I personally didn't consider getting insurance until I
started writing this book. It's not legally required, so I just
put it off, thinking that it wasn't essential and probably too
expensive. I know that insurance gets a bad name because
it's literally capitalising on fear, but I can honestly say that
now I've signed up I'm genuinely quite happy to pay £15 for
the peace of mind I have right now. Here's a quick rundown
of what you need to know about the types of insurance
available for freelancers:

PROFESSIONAL INDEMNITY INSURANCE
This covers you against the business risk of causing financial
loss to your client through your own negligence. I spoke to
Robert Hartley, who is one of the co-founders of Dinghy, an
insurance company specialising in policies for freelancers,

and he gave me an example of why you might need professional indemnity cover:

Imagine you were a graphic designer and you created a logo for a client and a year later a larger company says that your design breaches their trademark. They've also got the funds to take legal action. You could be held accountable for this and need to pay for lawyers and damages.

'You get your logo design put on your website, printed in a magazine, make loads of banners, and then suddenly someone says you've breached their trademark and you owe them £10,000. It's the designer of the logo who would need to pay this compensation,' says Robert. 'Something like this is an honest mistake. You didn't deliberately rip off this logo design and so professional indemnity cover will pay the compensation.'

Bear in mind, though, that this is only relevant when there has been some sort of financial loss. It can't be a client saying that they just don't like the logo!

PUBLIC LIABILITY INSURANCE
This offers protection against injury to other people or their belongings. It doesn't need to be a client; it can be anyone in the public who isn't you as long as it happens when you are working. Perfect for freelancers like me who work in public spaces like cafés, co-working spaces and libraries and live in fear of dropping a scalding hot chai latte over a stranger's laptop.

EQUIPMENT INSURANCE
Things like your laptop might be covered under your home insurance, but that's not always the case, so check with your

existing policy to find out where you stand. It's also worth noting that your home insurance might not cover items when you are using them outside of the house and some policies totally exclude business items anyway. I personally have worldwide cover on business equipment so that if my laptop ever breaks or is stolen, I can get a replacement ASAP.

CYBER INSURANCE

This is something that I don't have, but might be worth considering if you handle a lot of customer data.

'Say you visit a website and you accidentally download a ransomware virus and get an email saying you need to pay £500 or all the information on your computer will be deleted,' says Robert. 'The insurance company would help with that. If you hold a lot of customer data like addresses or bank details then you would want that protection.'

INCOME PROTECTION

For most freelancers, loss of income is a major concern. This type of insurance helps by providing you with an income in the event that you are unable to work due to long-term sickness or as a result of an accident. Policies will provide you with a percentage of your gross income for a set time or until retirement, depending on the terms.

HOW MUCH DOES IT COST?

There's no set rate for insurance policies as it depends on the cover you need as well as what kind of work you do. I currently pay about £15 a month for professional indemnity, public liability and equipment insurance, so that gives you an idea of what to expect.

> TIP: Look out for freelance specific insurers like Dinghy. They offer added benefits like Freelancer Assist, which gives you access to 24/7 helplines for legal matters, tax investigations and counselling. Dinghy also has a team of experts on-hand who will chase up late payments (over £200) on your behalf.

YOUR SPACE

Finding a good space in which to work may or may not be important to you. If you're a PR consultant, then a comfortable office chair and a moderately spacious desk is probably good enough. You might even start with just a smartphone writing emails from your living-room sofa. But those with more practical tasks are going to need a space that can accommodate tools and equipment.

Think about your potential clients and how you want to be perceived. Are you going to be having a lot of meetings? If so, is a coffee shop the best place to carry them out? I'm personally a huge fan of the coffee and cake meeting, as I like clients to know that we can relax around one another. I have no airs and graces, but that might not work for your business. Maybe your client is divulging sensitive information and therefore vulnerable in a busy environment. Maybe you're delivering training to small groups and need an entire room with catering and equipment to give a presentation. Maybe you're offering beauty treatments and you need a room with total privacy, running water, a waiting area and a receptionist. You can see from just these few examples that everyone's

It's worth a little forward planning to make sure that you can actually do your day-to-day tasks with relative ease.

needs are different, and so it's worth a little forward planning to make sure that you can actually do your day-to-day tasks with relative ease.

THE IMPORTANCE OF HAVING A DEDICATED SPACE

One of the major benefits of freelancing is also its biggest curse; you can work from anywhere. This means that the boundaries between your work and personal life can become blurry incredibly quickly, and in a way that you might not even notice. For example, say you work at your kitchen table, the place where you also eat your meals. At lunch time, do you eat while you work because you don't have a dedicated space to eat? Similarly, you might get into the habit of working from bed because you don't have a comfortable desk to sit at. Not only will this do some serious damage to your neck and back, but you could start to associate the bedroom with work and find it difficult to switch off and fall asleep at night. This is why you should at least give some prior consideration to where you want to work. You are going to be your own boss after all, so why not enjoy being in control for once?

WORK FROM HOME

If all you need to do your work is a quiet room, a laptop and an internet connection, then like most freelancers you can start your career working from home. It's the obvious solution because it doesn't cost anything other than the bills you already pay, although these may increase slightly, especially if you crank the heating up full blast and make twenty cups of tea before noon. But in general terms, using your home as your workspace is the most affordable option for most. If you do opt for this solution, here are some tips to help you set clear boundaries to maintain good mental health:

- Get up in the morning as though you were going to a regular job. Get showered, get dressed, leave the house if you want and walk around the block to create a 'commute'.
- Always take breaks away from your desk, ideally out of the house but, let's be honest, the sofa is just fine.
- Arrange your desk so it points away from potential distractions like the TV or the overflowing laundry basket.
- When you have a few hours to kill at the weekend, try not to automatically sit down at your desk. You wouldn't have used that time to go into the office when you had a traditional job, would you? Go watch Netflix, for crying out loud!

RENT A SPACE
Consider renting a room if you really need the space, but remember you'll need to be 100% sure that you can cover the cost, as you'll likely be tied into a contract that lasts several months if not an entire year.

CONSIDER CO-WORKING
There are tonnes of co-working spaces up for grabs these days, making use of city-centre buildings that put you right in the thick of it if that's what you need. You can normally pick from either a hot desk (just choose a desk and use it) or paying for a private office. Prices vary depending on location, perks (e.g. printing services, reception, free coffee) and how often you want to visit (daily, weekly, monthly, etc.). According a survey by Deskwanted, the average monthly

cost of a 'flexible desk' is $195 in the United States, €189 in Europe and £168 in the UK.[32] It's something that I've considered from time to time, but I've honestly never been able to justify the spend for the type of work I do. I have a perfectly fine home office that has all the perks I need. And by perks I mean the ability to wander around in my pyjamas singing Queen songs at the top of my lungs.

> TIP: If you just want a change of scenery without spending any money and don't care about the social aspect of talking to others, visit your local library and see if there is space available.

PAY AS YOU GO

There are plenty of spaces that have rooms for hire if you need to host one-off events or larger meetings. Many hotels, bars and cafés have private function rooms that you can reserve under the condition that your guests spend a certain amount on food and drinks.

There are also lots of freelancers organising their own co-working events, and Jessica Berry from Nottingham, UK did just this. She started off with a small group of fellow freelancers and has since gone on to launch an affordable membership scheme which allows people to sign up to get access to co-working one day a week starting at £30 per month. Look out for similar schemes in your area and if you can't find any, consider setting one up yourself. Such programmes are made easier by other services such as Dispace, an online platform designed to highlight empty spaces in cities that remote workers can use for co-working, meetings and events.

TOOLS OF THE TRADE

Keeping your expenses to a minimum is essential in the early days. My only 'start-up' costs were a laptop (which was actually a Christmas and birthday present combined from my long-suffering husband) and a few apps that cost less than £1. Here are a few things that you may (or may not) want to include in your freelancer starter kit, however, assuming you're going to be working from home:

- Laptop/desktop computer
- WiFi
- Smartphone
- Comfortable office chair
- Desk
- Printer
- Noticeboard
- Storage boxes/bookcase
- Stationery
- Website hosting

Here are some other things that may also cost you money:

- Computer software (e.g. Photoshop, Quickbooks)
- Technical support
- Hiring an accountant
- Travel and accommodation (trains, fuel, hotels)

- Special equipment (especially if you create your own physical products)
- Apps or services (e.g. social media scheduling apps)

And here's a bunch of costs that you'd better hope don't become a regular occurrence:

- Unexpected tax bills
- Legal advice
- Parking tickets
- Replacing a broken computer/phone/printer

And then there's these other purchases that you swore you didn't need but end up paying for anyway:

- Branding/snazzy logo design
- Business cards on the posh paper
- Marketing advice
- Ebooks
- Online courses

OTHER BORING THINGS TO NOTE

Gawd, here's the awful truth. Freelancing can be hella boring sometimes. In the past week alone I've fallen asleep at my desk at least twice while trying to carry out the basic task of finding the right type of insurance for my business. (Oh BTW, now is a good opportunity to let you in on a secret: I have no idea what I'm doing, and have learnt while writing this book that there are quite a few things that I could be doing better as part of my own OOO life.)

There are lots of nap-inducing aspects of being your own boss, and that's just all part of the job. One day, hopefully I'll be able to outsource those dreaded tasks to a friendly assistant who also keeps me motivated, makes me go to my dental check-ups and hands me a strong G&T every Friday at 5 pm (or earlier; I assume with my friendly assistant around we'll get our work done much earlier than usual), but until that sweet future is a reality, boring jobs are my sole responsibility. Here are a few other things that you might not know you need to keep on top of:

DATA SECURITY

If you're a business based in the EU, you need to comply with the General Data Protection Regulations. Over eighty countries now have their own privacy laws in place, so make sure you are following best practices in your own location. There are various aspects that you'll need to look at within your business relating to how you store and use other people's data, such as email addresses and financial details. There's also an associated fee with this (yay, more money), which depends on the size of your business. You can find out more at www.ico.org.uk.

From 25th May 2018, the Data Protection (Charges and Information) Regulations 2018 requires every organisation or sole trader who processes personal information to pay a data protection fee to the ICO, unless they are exempt.[33]

In America there isn't a federal-level data security law but there are some state-specific ones such as the Californian Consumer Privacy Act. You should check your government website depending on where in the world you're located.

HEALTH AND SAFETY

If your work poses a risk to others (e.g. you run a fairground ride), then you will need to adhere to health and safety laws. Depending on where you live there will also be other laws that apply to you if you hire employees (another reason to fly solo, if you ask me). The good news is that you don't need to comply with many health and safety laws if you're self-employed and working alone. This doesn't mean you should run with scissors in between meetings or start operating equipment after a few glasses of Malbec. I'm not going to pretend to know anything about health and safety, but I do want to point out the importance of making sure you don't cut corners when it comes to personal safety.

One example is the importance of a comfortable desk set-up. And no, this doesn't mean hooking up your espresso machine so that you can reach it from your bed while you crack on with answering emails. I suffer from a bad back as a result of years working in cafés where I was lugging boxes and stacking chairs every day. I thought the pain would improve when I went freelance, but I didn't realise that being hunched over a laptop for ten hours a day would make this pain even more excruciating.

After a few weeks at physio, my husband helped me pick out a proper office chair with arm and back support, as well as a monitor to make sure I was in the correct position when staring at my screen. I also paid a few quid for a little padded strip to keep my wrists from resting on the corner of the table. These are little things that often come as standard in offices but are worth considering as you set yourself up as a home-office dweller.

PAPERWORK

Having all the boring paperwork in place before you have any clients on your books is a super smart idea. It was not one that I personally implemented and I lived to regret it. Flying by the seat of your pants when it comes to some things is fine, but making sure your agreements are solid is something worth doing. Don't worry, I'll delve deeper into contracts, invoices and record-keeping in the next few chapters.

CHECKLIST

- Set up a website
- Register as a sole trader
- Look into insurance options
- Consider your workspace location and set-up
- Deal with the boring stuff

CHAPTER 9

TAX

Note: Everything in this chapter relates to UK law. If you're working outside of the UK, please visit your country's government website to find out how you should pay tax.

One of the things that a lot of freelancers get confused about is paying tax. I hear you!

Ninety-nine per cent of the self-employed people that I know made the leap because they are creative, full of ideas and buzzing with enthusiasm for their particular line of work. I know women who can stand up on a stage with a Britney-Bitch head mic and bang out a sixty-minute presentation to an audience of thousands. I know people who can go on national TV and talk about trauma they experienced as a child. But not one freelance friend of mine has ever said that they feel totally confident dealing with tax. (Apart from Julia, who you'll hear from later in this chapter – but she is a trained accountant so she has a very unfair advantage.)

The chances are you don't know much about paying tax as a freelancer, but you know what? That's normal! None of us (apart from Julia) knew how to do this stuff in the beginning, but it's honestly not as complicated as it seems. For one, you've got this book. But there's also plenty of information and support out there to help you ensure you've got everything under control.

WHAT IS TAX?

In the UK, you are legally required to pay income tax to the government. The amount you pay is based on how much you earn. If you have a contract of employment then this automatically comes out of your wage packet, but when you're self-employed you need to complete a tax return and pay a bill based on the profits you made in the last financial year. The process you go through to document this and calculate your tax bill is called Self Assessment. Make sure you're actually registered as a sole trader before you try to file your tax return, and don't try to register right before you need to submit, as there is a waiting time between setting up and being able to complete your first tax return.

WHEN DO I NEED TO DO MY TAX RETURN?

The UK tax year starts on 6th April and ends on 5th April the following year. You need to file your Self Assessment by 31st January. You also need to pay your tax bill on the same date. (At the very latest. Yes, there are fines if you're late.)

Example
So, if you set up a business in June 2018, your first tax return would include information based on your accounts

from the day you started trading until 5th April 2019. The deadline for submitting your tax return would be 31st January 2020. This is the final deadline, and payment is required on this date too, so do yourself a favour and submit it ahead of time.

After the tax year has ended you'll get an email inviting you (so charming) to submit your return. Ignore this email at your own risk. Yes, you technically have nine months to get it done, but raise your hand if every December you scream 'HOW IS IT CHRISTMAS ALREADY?' Christmas is a time for cheerful glee, obnoxious knitted jumpers and cinnamon-scented everything. It's not the time to be worrying about filing paperwork that ultimately results in a bill that you can't afford to pay. Complete your Self Assessment in April, May or June and at least you'll have a concrete idea of what you owe and ample time to set aside extra savings if you haven't done so already.

> TIP: Follow the month-end checklist in the Admin and Organisation chapter religiously to make completing your tax return easy peasy.

PAYMENTS ON ACCOUNT

These are advance payments towards your tax bill. I know, it's gross. You have to make two payments on account every year unless your last Self Assessment tax bill was less than £1,000 or you've already paid more than 80% of all the tax you owe, for example through your tax code or because your bank has already deducted interest on your savings.[34]

Each payment is half your previous year's tax bill and payments are due by midnight on 31st January and 31st July.

HOW SHOULD I SAVE FOR TAX?

You should save money for tax based on your estimated yearly salary. The threshold for tax-free allowance is the same as if you were in regular employment. It changes from year to year, but for the tax year 2019/20, the standard personal allowance was £12,500. You will pay income tax on anything you earn over that amount.

HOW MUCH TAX DO I NEED TO PAY?

You are required to pay 20% of your taxable income. So if you earnt £15,000 then you would only be taxed on £2,500 (because the first £12,500 is tax-free). You then take away any expenses and only pay tax on what's left because this is your profit. Say your expenses were £1,000 that year, you take that away from the £2,500 and you're left with £1,500. Your tax bill will be roughly 20% of £1,500 which is £300.

To summarise:
  Total income: £15,000
  Minus personal allowance: £12,500
  Minus expenses: £1,000
  Equals: £1,500
  20% of £1,500 is £300

This is by no means an exact figure for your final bill, but it's a good way to make an educated guess and take steps to set this aside in a savings account throughout the year so you're fully prepared. If you anticipate your tax bill to be over £1,000 then remember you'll need to put away an additional 50% in line with payments on account. This is why keeping records and looking at your month-end data is crucial to staying on top of your tax bill. Turn to page 161 to read my month-end paperwork routine.

DO I NEED AN ACCOUNTANT?

Full disclosure: I do not have an accountant. I know some freelancers who do and it works for them. My first tax return only accounted for seven months of income (I registered as self-employed in October and the tax year ends in April) and it will be no surprise to you that there wasn't much income to speak of. I estimated that my tax bill would be close to zero (it was around £100 if I remember correctly, which I don't) and when I asked around about how much it would cost to pay an accountant to complete my tax return for me, the figures were double or triple my estimated tax bill.

There is no doubt that this would have been money well spent (I sweated approximately 2.5 pints of bodily fluids as I muddled my way through my first tax return), but look, I couldn't afford it.

Maybe one day in the future I will outsource my accounting, but I actually quite enjoy filling out my spreadsheets every month and seeing in black and white how much I'm making and how much I'm spending. For some freelancers it's helpful to have your finger on the pulse when it comes to tax. It might stop you from lying awake at night when you've already mentally calculated how much you need to save in the next year. For others, outsourcing to an accountant is exactly what they need.

TIPS ON COMPLETING YOUR SELF ASSESSMENT

- Do your accounts at the end of every month using a spreadsheet to record your income and expenses. This will make the process so much easier.
- Visit the gov.uk YouTube channel to watch advice videos on how to complete each section.
- Have your P60 to hand if you were employed.
- Do it in stages if it stresses you out. You can fill out sections and then save it and go back to it later.
- If you are completely terrified, hire an accountant to do it for you.

VAT

Value Added Tax is something that adds to the cost of lots of things we buy every day, and some businesses are required to collect it on things they sell. If you do, you send that extra money to HMRC. You can also claim back any VAT that you pay on business supplies.

You are legally obliged to register for VAT if:

- you expect your VAT-taxable turnover to be more than £85,000 in the next thirty-day period
- your business had a VAT taxable turnover of more than £85,000 over the last twelve months

You might also need to register in some other cases, depending on the kinds of goods or services you sell and where you sell them.[35]

CLAIMING EXPENSES

When I started out as a freelancer I didn't think I'd have many expenses to claim. I didn't drive, I didn't rent office space, I didn't need anything other than a laptop, an internet connection and unlimited access to instant coffee to get the work done. But once I started keeping receipts and tracking what I spent every month, I realised that I was investing a fair chunk of money in my business that could be claimed as expenses.

Here's what I claim as expenses every single month:

- Subscription to Canva (website for making artwork like logos, etc)
- Subscription to Buffer (social media scheduler)
- Web hosting
- Gmail business
- Books
- Podcast hosting service
- Travel costs for meetings and networking events
- Postage

And here's a list of things that crop up a few times a year:

- Accommodation when I'm at an event, doing a speaking gig or meeting a client
- Tickets for networking events

If you worked for a company that values its employees you would be offered opportunities to work on your training and development, so as your own boss you should try to do this too.

- Outsourcing technical help for my website
- Business cards
- Flyers

Most months, I also claim for things like notebooks, pencils and printer ink. Sure, they don't cost the earth, but when you add it up over a year it can amount to hundreds or even thousands of pounds, especially if you love Paperchase as much as I do. If you've already spent that money then you'd be daft not to claim it back, because if you don't you're increasing the amount you'll need to pay in tax. And no one wants to make their tax bill bigger than it needs to be, trust me.

The best thing about expenses for me is that it makes me feel a lot better about those business costs that feel a bit luxurious. Building a business means that you should be continually working on improving how it functions, and if you're a sole trader then that means investing in yourself. If you worked for a company that values its employees you would be offered opportunities to work on your training and development, so as your own boss you should try to do this too.

I love nothing more than finding a little bit of extra money in my account and spending it on a few hours of one-to-one business coaching, and knowing that I can claim it as an expense makes it feel even more worthwhile. Bear in mind that not all training can be claimed as a business expense, so visit the HMRC website to make sure you adhere to government guidelines.

If you work from home you may be able to claim a proportion of your costs for things like:

- Heating
- Electricity
- Council Tax
- Mortgage interest or rent
- Internet and telephone use

You can either calculate this as a percentage or use a flat rate. Both of these are explained in more detail on www.gov. uk, where you can use the simplified expenses checker to find out which is best for your business.

TIP: Keep business receipts in a separate section of your purse and in a designated folder on your email account. This makes them easy to find at the end of the month.

Q&A WITH JULIA DAY

Julia Day is a fully trained accountant and has consulted with me on this chapter to make sure I haven't told you any porky pies. She's also the founder of The Independent Girls Collective, an online membership site that delivers monthly courses and resources based around issues that us freelancers have to deal with on the regular such as tax, contracts, etc. She's even got a course called 'mastering tax' which is perfect for anyone who wants to learn more about the topic. Here are the answers to the most frequently asked questions on tax, record-keeping and, of course, claiming coffee as an expense:

DO FREELANCERS NEED AN ACCOUNTANT?
If you're a sole trader, you probably don't need one because your accounts are probably pretty straightforward. Bear in mind that if your accountant messes up your tax return (yes, it happens!) it will come back on you not them, because you're the person paying the tax. HMRC can still fine you even if you're using an accountant, so having one doesn't make your tax return fool-proof.

DO I NEED TO PAY NATIONAL INSURANCE?
If you earn under a certain amount then you don't need to pay National Insurance. However, your payments will go towards things like benefits and a state pension. I've had family who were self-employed for a bit and then couldn't claim benefits at a later date as a result. It's not a huge amount of money so I would say always pay National Insurance if you get the option.

WHAT HAPPENS IF I GET A MASSIVE UNEXPECTED TAX BILL AND I DON'T HAVE THE MONEY TO PAY IT?
Get in touch with HMRC and you can pay in instalments. They will add on a bit of interest but they are flexible and

helpful with setting this up. They *want* you to be able to pay what you owe.

HOW DO I PAY BACK MY STUDENT LOAN?

When you do your tax return they will ask if you were a student during certain dates. You pay a percentage of what you owe if you earn over a certain amount. As long as you say you were a student when you fill out your tax return, it will all be calculated for you and you'll repay it slowly over time.

WHAT IS 'MAKING TAX DIGITAL'?

It's a new scheme by HMRC which means all tax returns have to be done online. Some people still do a paper tax return but that's going to be phased out in the future, but they keep putting it back, so I'm not sure when it will come into effect. You'll do a tax return every quarter instead of every year which will make things easier as you'll have small amounts to pay on a more regular basis. It means there should be fewer surprises for you along the way! You will need to use software that works with HMRC but they are developing free software that everyone can use.

HOW LONG DO I NEED TO KEEP RECORDS?

Six years. However, you don't need paper copies, you just need records of some sort, so digital is fine. You also don't need to keep physical receipts – just take pictures and store them digitally. And there's no need to upload any documents unless you earn over a certain amount, so filling out a tax return is a lot simpler than you think!

CAN I CLAIM COFFEE AS AN EXPENSE?

You can only claim it if you're buying it because you're working outside of your usual routine, for example at a conference or meeting a client. However you can't claim for a client's meal or coffee, only your own.

DO I NEED A BUSINESS BANK ACCOUNT?

No, but I highly recommend it because it keeps everything separate. It's also good because you can hook it up to your accounting software such as QuickBooks or Xero and basically every month you just go through your statement and make sure everything is right. Some banks say you can't use current accounts for business, though, so it's best to check. Coming from the corporate world it was drummed into me to have a business bank account. If you're running a limited company, you do legally need a business bank account.

TAKE EVERYTHING I SAY WITH A PINCH OF SALT (AND GOVERNMENT GUIDELINES)

This is not a book about tax (thank god, because this has been a struggle to write) so please take this chapter as it was intended, as a brief overview. A beginner's guide. I'm still getting to grips with tax myself and although my experience has been relatively simple (so far), everyone's business requirements are totally unique. If in doubt, pay an accountant to look at your finances and do it sooner rather than later.

I've spent way too long wondering if this chapter was good enough to publish. I've gone down rabbit holes, heard horror stories and read every single page of the HMRC website when it comes to paying income tax as a freelancer. I've over-complicated it in my head, and I lie awake worrying that I've over-simplified it here. I've probably missed something out that could apply to your specific set of circumstances, but I'm not here to hold your hand and do the work for you. If you are serious about being a freelancer then you will take this chapter as a jumping-off point, a signpost to your personal path which you will need to navigate as best you see fit. But when I spoke to my straight-talking, beautiful friend Sinead Latham, who manages to work full-time, freelance at night and still be a kick-ass mother, mate and all-round wonder woman, she said I could have deleted this entire chapter and replaced it with one sentence: 'Tax. Pay it. The end.' She's super smart.

CHECKLIST

- Put money aside (in a separate account) every month for taxes so you don't get caught out at the end of the year.
- Complete your Self Assessment as soon as the tax year ends. This will give you a clear figure and well over six months to make sure you have the money to pay your bill.
- Keep receipts to claim eligible purchases as business expenses.

CHAPTER 10

GETTING YOUR FIRST CLIENT

So you've decided you wanna give this freelance thing a bash and you're all fired up and ready to go. But how does one actually *get* going? Setting up as a sole trader is one thing, but actually going out and getting clients is another. I absolutely love talking to other freelancers to find out how they get their clients because there's no one set way that works for everyone. Many freelancers get their first client by accident. Sometimes an opportunity falls into their lap that is just too good to turn down. Others are handed work by previous employers. Others work for free and end up with a paid gig as a result. (See page 118 for some real-life examples.)

If you were hoping for a paint-by-numbers-style guide to getting your first client, then I hate to burst your bubble, but you won't find that here. The reality is that potential clients are everywhere and there are a million ways you can seek them out. All around you there are family members, friends, colleagues, ex-bosses and old flatmates who know someone who knows someone who wants what you're selling. This chapter will give you various examples of how to make the most of your existing network and tap into new ones, all the while flying your freelance flag with pride.

Because if you wave it for long enough, someone is bound to notice you, I promise.

REAL-LIFE EXAMPLES OF HOW FREELANCERS GOT THEIR FIRST CLIENT

'My boyfriend's friend was a sci-fi writer and he suggested I do his book cover. My best friend's friend ran a Jewish summer camp, and I offered to redesign their brochure. I cold-called my favourite digital designer in NYC to get an internship, the bill for which cost me £50. It paid off as I got the internship, and afterwards they offered me a freelance gig doing ATM screen UX design research.' – Kate

'My first client was my previous employer, but my first completely new client was a referral from the person who was my manager on my university placement year fifteen years earlier. The power of reputation and your network providing referrals!' – Luan

'I got mine by looking on Facebook marketplace for jobs. I was looking around the London area and it just popped up!' – Vee

'I started out web designing and spent the first few hours of my day looking for poorly made websites. I'd politely email the owners to offer my assistance and it worked well!' – Aimee

'I broke my ankle the week I became a freelancer! After a few days struggling with crutches I went online and found a hands-free crutch. It was so amazing I contacted

---

the CEO to tell him more people needed to know about it. He was my first new client and I still work with him.' – Natasha

'Somebody put a poster to design their wedding dress with all those little snippets of paper dangling off the bottom with her phone number.' – Charlotte

'I was a painter and decorator, broke my back, started planning a photo calendar from my hospital bed – suggested by a mate – sold 350 in six weeks, which paid the mortgage for nearly two months and I became a full-time photographer and videographer from then on.' – Charlie

'Through my random post on LinkedIn with a photo doing open mic in comedy club I got contacted by an international conference organiser who'd lost their comedian and asked me, on a five-day notice. Didn't think they'd like me but they did and that's how I'm a corporate event comedian.' – Beatrice

HAVE EXAMPLES OF YOUR WORK READY

Before you go chasing clients, think about how you're going to prove to them that you have the skills required to carry out the work. I know if I was handing over money to a photographer I'd want to see some bangin' examples of their images when I click on their website. When I went looking for a business coach, I read testimonials from previous clients to see what kind of results I could expect. When I'm scoping out a new hairdresser, the first thing I do is head to their Instagram account to see pictures of their most recent updos and blow dries. When you're starting out you need to build up a body of work to show to potential customers that you can do the thing that they're paying you to do.

WHAT IF YOU HAVE NO EXAMPLES OF YOUR WORK?

But how, you ask, do you show examples of your work if you haven't had any clients? Well, that depends entirely on the nature of your work. When I started out I didn't realise that I was going to be a freelance writer, but it turns out that having a blog was my way of creating an online portfolio of my work. I didn't have any paying clients, but I had hundreds of examples of my writing published on my own website. If you're an artist, don't wait for someone to commission you. Make art first and show people what you can do, otherwise they'll never know what you're capable of. If you're a marketing guru, ask another small business if you can give them a consultancy package for free and then use the results as a case study to put on your website. Too many freelancers waste time feeling entitled to paying clients before they've got some experience under their belt, so bite the bullet and start doing your thing. Putting in that hard work at the beginning will pay off in the long run.

TIP: Consider doing a skill swap with another budding freelancer so that you can both build up your portfolio. For example, an editor might work on an eBook for a marketing strategist in exchange for a one-to-one coaching session.

WORKING FOR FREE

I could write an entire book on the subject of working for free, and I could fall on either side of the argument depending on my mood that day. Working for free is something that I've done at various stages throughout my career (and still do on occasion) for various reasons. I've written for websites to show that my work is good enough to be published somewhere other than my blog. I've spoken at events to raise my profile and promote my books. I've trained people on how to use Pinterest to see if that was a skill I wanted to add to my repertoire. But working for free is a privilege that I have been granted because I have always been able to do so and still afford to pay my bills. This means that people who can't afford to work for free might be missing out on opportunities that could further their career and get them more clients, and that makes me mad.

According to IPSE, half of all freelancers have reported being asked to work for free, and 43% have completed jobs for no pay.[36] There's an ongoing joke in the world of freelancing that you can't pay your bills with 'exposure', which is what most companies claim you'll get when you work for free. But here's the thing, you might get a little bit of traction, but there's no guarantee it will lead to paid work. In fact, the company you've just provided the service for probably has very little respect for the work you actually do.

Digital marketing coach Alice Benham spoke to me about how she believes that putting value on what you offer has a direct impact on the quality of your work. She says,

> *From my point of view any clients who have paid full price have a better attitude. All of my bad clients have been ones who have got it*

Don't make a habit of working for free.

discounted or for free. I think it says a lot about someone's attitude when they are willing to pay for a service. I have such a better relationship with every single one of my clients because I know that they are paying a price that I genuinely know is fair for what my time is worth, and the value they are getting.

I've also experienced the horror of working for free and the client expecting me to bend over backwards, sometimes even be out of pocket in order to achieve the end result. My advice is that if you do choose to work for free, make sure that you are getting something that money can't buy in return. Whether it's exposure, experience, customer testimonials or the chance to make some priceless connections, get in, do the job, get out and then move on. And don't make a habit of working for free.

THE CHALKBOARD METHOD™[37]

I've read countless self-help books in my time but the one thing that continues to boggle my mind is the act of visualising. Yup, we're about to get a bit woo woo – you've been warned. Want to make your first million? Visualise it. Want to do a TED talk? Visualise it. Want to be one of those people who can buy a sharing bag of Maltesers and, you know, actually share it? Visualise. It.

It's something that takes practice and, honestly, it's not for everyone. But when it comes to earning enough money to pay your bills, I think you should put your woo woo prejudice to one side for just a minute and give this one a go. Because it's pretty practical and doesn't involve closing your eyes or burning sage in every corner of your home.

To the best of my knowledge, The Chalkboard Method was first mentioned on the Being Boss podcast. In fact, go listen to episode #79 if you want the full scoop. It's essentially a way of goal-setting that involves (you guessed it) a chalkboard. Instead of simply *thinking* that you would like five new clients, you make it visual. You actually create a space in your life for those five clients.

I know what you're thinking – how do you create an 'empty space'? Well, get a chalkboard (or whiteboard, or piece of paper... whatever works) and write the heading 'CLIENTS'. Underneath it make five spaces that you will fill with clients when you secure them. Draw an actual space. I like to draw a big square, and when I have the client I write their name in the box. Repeat this exercise three times so that you have a quarterly plan broken down into monthly goals. I've also used this technique to book speaking gigs, sell event tickets and get features commissioned for magazines. Placing this chalkboard in a prominent place where you can see it every day is powerful. I mean it. Prop it up above your desk so that it subconsciously seeps into your peripheral vision as you work.

Although this is a general goal-setting tool, I find it wildly successful when it comes to financial goals. When it gets to halfway through the month and you realise you've still got multiple slots to fill on your chalkboard, you'll be amazed at how focused you can become. You start sending out emails, phoning up past clients, posting more on social media. You'll find that ideas and new leads will seemingly pop up out of thin air. Try it.

NETWORKING

I got my first real client without actually looking for work.
Lucky me, right? If that was always the case I'd be a feckin'
millionaire but, alas, I still need to pop into the Poundshop
on the regular when my bank account is out of shape.
Finding customers is H A R D. And one thing that just can't
be avoided if you want to earn money as a freelancer is
the power of networking. Online. Offline. Both valid, both
essential, if you ask me.

I've had some interesting interactions with potential clients
on social media. I've had my fair share of 'exciting business
opportunities' slide into my DMs that have turned out to be
pyramid schemes, multi-level marketing schemes (MLMs) or
in one slightly terrifying turn of events an invitation to receive
payments in exchange for some 'interesting', shall we say,
homemade video content. But I've also found some lucrative
opportunities online too.

COLD EMAILING

When I first started freelance writing I had one major client,
but I wanted to broaden my horizons in the journalism
world. I spent a day trawling through Twitter accounts
to find the editors of magazines and websites who were
regularly publishing mental health content and I came across
Happiful Magazine. The mental health publication was in
its infancy – I believe at that point they had only printed a
handful of issues and, from memory, they didn't have a big
following on social media. But I found the head of content
and sent her a message asking if they were accepting pitches.
To my surprise (editors aren't known for responding to DMs,
presumably because they get so many) she said that I had

contacted her at just the right time as they were actively looking to connect with freelance writers. I pointed her in the direction of my blog and my published work and the next day we were on the phone discussing features and rates. Several years later, *Happiful Magazine* is one of my favourite clients, because they've been with me since the beginning. I'm not saying that every single conversation you have online is going to end up a success story, but this is one example of how putting yourself out there can lead to long-term clients.

MAKING PALS

When I moved to Birmingham in 2016, I only knew a handful of people. I missed Glasgow and the friends that I had grown up with, but I knew that if we were putting roots down in a new city then I was going to have to make some acquaintances.

I turned up to blogging events on my own, interjected myself into people's lives and asked them out for coffee on the regular. For a while, I even hosted my own events in a bid to create a bit of a mental health community in my area. Each event featured a few speakers who would tell their story to encourage conversation and inspire people.

It was one of these speakers – Kirsty Hulse – who came along to talk about her book *The Future is Freelance* and captured my little heart. I'm not going to go on a vomit-inducing spiel about how much I love this woman, but just know that she has played a major part (even though she wouldn't admit it) in my creating a profitable business. Talking to her and hearing her success story as a twenty-something woman in tech was inspiring, and I felt magnetically drawn to soak up every last drop of knowledge she had to share. How has this led to more clients for me? There are a number of examples:

1 She has hired me personally to do freelance work for her business

2 She has recommended me as a speaker

3 She coached me on how to overcome the anxiety of public speaking and have confidence on stage

4 She has point-blank FORCED me to increase my prices, which led to my highest paying jobs as a freelancer

She's also just a hugely funny and compassionate person. Go read her book.

Sometimes the benefits of networking are obvious. You speak to a person and they hire you. But sometimes the ripple effects of networking aren't visible for months or even years in the future. There's no way to predict which conversations will lead to business connections, genuine friendships or a blend of both. The secret is to simply start talking.

INDUSTRY EVENTS

Being present at conferences that bring your industry out in force might be something that helps you find more clients. As a freelance journalist for example, it might seem pointless for me to spend a day talking to other writers. None of them are going to commission me to write for their magazine, are they? Probably not. But they can share knowledge. And they DO. We all do. I'm not saying that I share my best tips with every budding journalist I meet, but the friendly ones, the ones who give as much as they take, those people are the ones I let in on how I make ends meet.

CO-WORKING

I'm on the fence about co-working because I find it the opposite of conducive to productivity. It makes my output non-existent. Word count: zero. Emails pile up as I drink too much coffee and gossip with friends. But as a way to get more clients? Potentially helpful, especially if you offer services that your co-workers might benefit from. I sold a few copies of my books and tickets to events that I've hosted to people I've worked with, and I know lots of other freelancers who get word-of-mouth recommendations through co-working.

KEEPING CLIENTS

Maintaining clients is important because repeat business is much easier to source than new business, and satisfied customers are likely to recommend you to a friend or colleague.

When I was promoted to manager of a café at the tender age of twenty-one, I had a lot to learn. But one thing I was dead cert on was damage control. Having undiagnosed anxiety meant that I was constantly worried about making things right before they went wrong, essential assuming that the sh*t was about to hit the fan at any given moment. If customer service was affected, then that led to complaints, refunds and a loss of income, which would mean a bollocking from my area manager, which as a chronic people-pleaser I avoided at all costs. I like to think that my work history (as much as I hated it at the time) has shown me how to keep clients happy, and keep them coming back time and time again. So here are some tips on how to keep your existing clients feeling happy, valued and coming back for more:

COMMUNICATE

No one likes to be ignored, especially if they're paying for your time. Make sure everything you say is polite, friendly and crystal-clear. Email is great for keeping track of deadlines or tasks to be completed, but keep them short and to the point. No one wants to read your life story or what you were up to on your holidays. For complex conversations, use phone or video calls. You'll always achieve way more in a fifteen-minute conversation than you would over an email that takes the same amount of time to write.

KNOW YOUR STUFF

If you don't know the answer to something, be honest. Lying about your abilities will only lead to disgruntled clients who feel they've been duped. Say something like, 'That's not my area of expertise, but let me look into it', then do some research. Alternatively, recommend someone else who you trust. If there is a gap in your knowledge that is highlighted more than once, consider investing in some training to improve your skill set or find another freelancer you can pay to do the task for you.

BE REALISTIC

It can be super-tempting to promise prospective clients the world before they sign on the dotted line, especially in the beginning when you're hearing nothing but crickets in your inbox. Try your very best to be realistic about what you can provide for your paying customers and don't get their hopes up if you're not 100% certain you can deliver. I made this mistake by taking on clients who wanted help with Instagram. I'm more than qualified to deliver the work, but I didn't realise that people were expecting me to find them thousands of followers out of thin air. I know that it takes time (a lot of it) to build a genuine audience online, but clients hired me thinking that paying me a few hundred quid a month would make them Insta-famous. Now, I make it very clear what results clients can expect from the outset.

MEET YOUR DEADLINES

My husband worked in a mobile phone store when he was a student, and when I was bored I would go into the shop and wait for him to finish up his shift. I once watched him serve a customer who had a faulty phone, and they were going through the process of sending it to the warehouse to be repaired. My husband got everything sorted and sent the customer away relatively happy, and said that he could expect his phone to be fixed within two weeks. 'That's ages, isn't it?' I said to my husband after the customer was out of earshot. 'Two weeks to get your phone repaired?' To which he replied, 'It will be back within five days, they always are. We're trained to under-promise and over-deliver.' The lesson? Set long deadlines and deliver work ahead of time. It just looks good.

MULTIPLE INCOME STREAMS

There's nothing better than securing a big client on your books. Regular money coming in every month? Sweet! But before you upgrade your gin subscription box and order those Dr Martens you've been eyeing up for months, remember that relying on one major client comes with risks. The freelance life means that you can live a life of freedom, no employment contracts and no boss. But this also means that clients can cut you loose at any moment. Without any notice, depending on the terms of your contract.

One way to avoid this inevitable event having a major impact on your bank balance is to have multiple income streams. Over the years I've made ends meet by blogging, scheduling Tweets, writing for magazines, delivering social media training, public speaking and even doing PR for friends. Although I don't love each thing equally I'm grateful to have had them on the back burner, especially in the beginning when the website that normally commissioned the majority of my features had a reshuffle, and the editor who I was on good terms with moved on to another job. Under the new editor, all of my pitches were rejected – and I mean *all* of them – so I simply changed my focus from pitching to the social media side of my business. I also organised a few events and started building up my connections with new editors to make sure that when this happened again, I'd have plenty of places to look for income.

To build new revenue streams for your own business, begin by writing a list of every job you've ever had. Then make a note of all the different skills you used for each particular role. Also write down any subjects that you were passionate about when you were at school and/or university. Finally, think about the things that seem to come naturally to you but that the average person tends to find difficult e.g. public speaking, photography, fashion styling, cooking. Depending on your career history you should now have a list of multiple skills that can be transferable to your current business in ways you've not previously considered.

CHECKLIST

- Talk to everyone you meet about what you do as a freelancer. You never know where your first client is lurking.
- Make sure you have a few examples of your work to show prospective clients.
- Network, both online and offline.
- Be nice to your clients!
- Consider multiple income streams to protect you from unexpected dry spells.

CHAPTER 11

GETTING PAID

I've experimented with lots of different ways of figuring out how much to charge for my services and, to be honest, there are no hard-and-fast rules. What worked for me last year might not feel right anymore, and with many different strings to my bow (see 'Multiple income streams' in the previous chapter), one rule doesn't apply to every part of my business. For example, I might charge a client an hourly rate for copyediting, but when it comes to speaking, I can't do that. I may only be speaking for thirty minutes, but charging for half an hour of my time would be ludicrous. Instead, I have a set fee that takes lots of things into account, such as travel, preparation, training and experience.

What follows in this chapter isn't a formula on how to set your prices. Instead I've included the thought process behind tried-and-tested pricing structures so that you can pick the one that's right for you. I'll also explain why you probably need to charge more than you think. Remember, your prices aren't set in stone, so don't be afraid to take advantage of the freelancing model and change your rates to see what works best.

You've invested time in being good at what you do, potentially years of training and experience too. Make sure you're paid accordingly.

YOU DESERVE IT

First things first, I need you to accept that you are worthy of being paid for your work. This isn't about you being the leading artist/editor/virtual assistant in your industry or being head and shoulders above the rest. There will always be someone better (and worse) at doing what you do, but that's irrelevant. It's not about being cocky or feeling entitled to large sums of money; it's about believing that you should be paid fairly for providing something of value to another person.

It can be really hard to even contemplate asking for money for what you do, especially when you're first starting out and you're lacking in confidence (and clients). But you've got to believe that what you have is of value to other people and set your prices accordingly. If might be easy for you to design a website, but the reality is that most people haven't got a clue where to start. People are paying you because things come easy to you, because you have a skill or assets that can help them. I like to call this the knowledge tax.

As video director Davy Greenberg so succinctly put in his 2019 viral tweet, 'If I do a job in 30 minutes it's because I spent 10 years learning how to do that in 30 minutes. You owe me for the years, not the minutes.'

You get to charge extra because you have the knowledge to do something that your client can't (or doesn't want to) do themselves. You've invested time in being good at what you do, potentially years of training and experience too. Make sure you're paid accordingly.

Now that's cleared up, here are some different types of rates…

HOURLY RATE

This is where most people start when it comes to charging for their time, but beware: you may think that £20 an hour sounds good (after years of working for minimum wage, I certainly did), but remember within that amount you still need to cover overheads such as tax, insurance, your wages, stationery, travel, etc. And are you basing this on a forty-hour week? Can you guarantee you'll get enough work to fill up that time? Remember that even if you agree to work on client projects for a certain number of hours per week, they are probably (definitely) going to throw some ad-hoc (annoying) tasks your way from time to time. Make sure you are clear from the outset that any of these extra jobs will be billable. The trouble here is that some of these little jobs might only take ten minutes. **Do not bill for ten minutes!** Bill for the full hour or, even better, charge for a half-day. Which leads me on to...

DAY RATE

One of my friends runs a video production company and he says that half-days were eating up too much of their time. Heading out to film a video for half a day would always take longer than anticipated and by the time the team travel to and from the shoot, load and unload all the cameras, lighting and whatever other fancy kit videographers use, the rest of the day was a write-off. This meant that they were unavailable to take on other work that day, which was affecting their bottom line. Now, they only offer a full day of work, meaning that their time is spent more effectively.

PROJECT-BY-PROJECT BASIS

If you work on more complex projects that take more time and work, then it might be worth customising your pricing based on each client's requirements. For example, will you need to work on-site for a portion of the time? You might need to include travel and accommodation if that's the case. Are you going to need to outsource some tasks to specialists? Then you'll need to include that cost too. Are you supplying ongoing support that can't be charged hourly (e.g. troubleshooting via email for a few weeks after completion)? If so, you need to factor that in with your pricing. With these types of jobs the fees can rack up quickly, but breaking down all your charges and itemising each one can provide clarity to the client as well as demonstrate the value you'll be bringing to the table. If you're erring on the side of caution with your figures, I would always say to over-estimate how many hours or days that you think it will take to get the work done. There are always unforeseen roadblocks, people regularly push back deadlines and quite often (I'm sorry to say) change the goalposts as time goes on. With these projects, consider asking for half of the money upfront or sending an invoice on a monthly basis to make sure you're paid accordingly.

MONTHLY RETAINER

If you're doing something on a regular basis, it might be a good idea to suggest a monthly retainer fee. I do this with a few clients as I manage their email newsletters, blog content and social media profiles. As this is an ongoing job it makes sense to have a set fee every month, and it works well for me. The clients know that they won't receive an unexpectedly huge invoice at the end of the month and I know that I've got a guaranteed amount of money coming in every four weeks, which is a godsend when there isn't any other work on the horizon! Some experts suggest adding 20% to your hourly rate to ensure you make a profit (which is what we all want, right?).

HOW TO COME UP WITH A FIGURE

When I first started charging an hourly rate, I didn't think very much of myself. I'd been making sandwiches for a living for a few years and scraping by on £7 per hour and free food and coffees to make the day feel a little less dreary. So when I had to come up with a figure to charge for my services, I didn't feel worthy of asking for very much at all. I charged £10 per hour.

Several years later I upped that to £20 per hour, and I've increased it yet again since then. I did some research into what other people were charging and also thought about how much I would realistically like to earn every month. Say for example you want to earn £3,000 per month. Great, now how many hours would you like to work in that month? If the answer is 120 hours (thirty hours per week), then you would need to charge £25 per hour. (Bear in mind that this is all before tax, so you would lose a certain percentage of this to the government.) Instead of working backwards thinking about hours worked, maybe consider how many days you would like to work, or how many clients you can comfortably work with, or how many products you would need to sell to make up that income. The Chalkboard Method™ (see page 123) is great for this. Remember that just because the typical working week consists of five days, this doesn't necessarily mean you can dedicate five days to doing paid work. You'll need time to do the work that doesn't pay (in a direct sense anyway) such as sending invoices, implementing marketing campaigns, meeting with potential clients, etc. As a rule of thumb I would assume that at least one day week will be required for various freelancer-related tasks and then take it from there.

TIP: Talk to other freelancers and ask if they would give you a ballpark figure about what they charge. Do this with lots of people, not just one or two, because the chances are that they could be under- or over-charging for their services! When I increased my rates recently, I asked for input in a freelancer Facebook group and people were more than happy to tell me their hourly rate.

PERCEIVED VALUE

Marketing genius Seth Godin once wrote that the goal in selling is to make sure that what you sell is **irreplaceable**, **essential** and **priceless**.

'If you are all three, then you have pricing power. When the price charged is up to you, when you have the power to set the price, there is a line out the door and you can use pricing as a signalling mechanism, not merely a way to make a living.'[38]

It's really hard to be confident in charging more for what you do. I feel that hard, and struggle on the daily when I have to tell people what my rates are. But the truth is that people can either afford you or they can't. The price tag you put on your services sends a signal to customers and communicates the quality of the work you're going to do. When people are willing to put down cold hard cash it means that they're serious too, so it ultimately builds this amazing level of trust between you both that means your relationship is based on strong foundations.

I picked the brain of marketing coach Alice Benham who has made a conscious decision with her own pricing. She says:

Pricing plays a huge subconscious role in your business and it's something that we think people care about more than they do. There was a direct correlation for me between the moment I started charging what my time is actually worth and the moment I actually started getting booked with clients. I see businesses doing £10 off a £200 package deal and I think, If someone is going to spend £200, that tenner off isn't going to make a difference. People appreciate transparency.

PACKAGES

If you offer lots of different services that all come under one theme, it can be helpful to create packages. For example, a personal trainer may offer workout plans, nutritional advice, exercise sessions and maybe even mindset coaching. To sell these individually, you could create three packages. One on workouts, one on nutrition and one on mindset. You could even create the 'ultimate' package which combines elements of all three. Similarly, if you know that your work needs multiple purchases to create greater impact (e.g. a business coach might want to sell multiple sessions instead of just one), this is where packages can help.

Consider the rule of three when creating your packages. Consumers like to have freedom of choice, but too many options can be off-putting. Offering three packages at different price points (a bargain, an affordable amount and a considered investment) gives everyone a choice. As you've probably already guessed, a lot of people will opt for the middle package. This is known by psychologists as the 'centre-stage effect',[39] which suggests that the location of a product between two others has an impact on purchase decisions.

There will of course come a time when you'll be able to charge more for your services as you gain experience in your field. Head to page 225 to find out more about how to ask for more money.

CHECKLIST

- Acknowledge that you deserve to be paid a fair rate for the services you provide.
- Talk to other freelancers to get an idea of what the current going rate is for what you're selling.
- Start with a larger financial goal and work backwards based on the number of projects/hours you have in mind.
- Consider your overheads when you come up with a figure.
- Try creating packages to give customers a variety of options to choose from.
- Think about the kind of customers you want your pricing to attract.

CHAPTER 12

MANAGING YOUR MONEY

Getting money into your account is one thing, but how do you make sure that you're in control? I've been known to check my bank balance on an hourly basis while I wait patiently for invoices to be paid, in the hope that I can go on an elaborate shopping spree later to indulge in lavish luxuries such as bread and washing powder. But that's not what I want your (or my) life to be like. Sure, checking your balance is way healthier than not checking it at all, but it's much more relaxing to know that you're not living hand-to-mouth every thirty days. With that in mind, may I present:

7 WAYS TO STAY ON TOP OF YOUR FINANCES

1. HAVE A BUFFER FUND

Assume that things are going to go wrong at some point. There will be late invoices; there will be unforeseen charges; there will be late-night Uber Eats. Creating a buffer fund for emergencies is an excellent idea. Even if it's just a few hundred quid, you'll thank me later. This should be separate from your tax savings, because obviously they're for tax. If you're not earning enough money to save, then go back to Chapter 11 and think about your rates. Spend some time looking at your overheads and be realistic about how much you need to charge in order to have some left over for savings, then implement this rate for new customers. (Head to Chapter 17 for guidance on how to raise your rates with people who are already on your books.)

2. SORT OUT YOUR BANK ACCOUNTS

If you haven't got it already, set up internet banking for your existing accounts. Having instant access to your financial situation is a godsend when you're still getting to grips with managing your business money. The easiest way to save is to have different accounts for tax and savings. There are several new bank accounts that allow you to set up saving pots for different needs such as tax, haircuts, Christmas, wedding, etc., such as Monzo.

3. HAVE A MONTHLY MONEY DATE

Get your highlighter out and pick a day at the start of the month to reflect on your finances over the past thirty days. Use this time to do your month-end admin list (more details in the next chapter) and take stock of what you've spent and what you've earnt. If you use accounting software like Quickbooks then make use of the reporting tools. Use this data to adjust any plans you have and set new goals if required. (Refer back to the Chalkboard Method in Chapter 10 for further guidance.)

Paying yourself a regular income is essential.

4. AUTOMATE

Take the thinking out of your finances by setting up direct debits for all your regular payments. Twenty-nine per cent of people surveyed by the Association of Independent Professionals and the Self-Employed (IPSE) listed invoice processing as 'a task which could otherwise be spent on winning or completing new work'[40] – and they're not wrong. Consider using an automated invoicing tool such as Xero or Quickbooks to send out invoices and late payment reminders.

5. INCREASE YOUR RATES

I'm not saying that you should charge ludicrous amounts for your work, but chances are if you're worried about money, then you're undercharging. (See page 225 for more on this.)

6. PAY YOURSELF A SALARY

Paying yourself a regular income is essential, especially if you find the variable cashflow situation hard to deal with. It can be tempting to overspend when you have a good month, but remember that there will be quiet months in the future where your bank balance needs a little boost. To avoid the feast-and-famine scenario, pay yourself a sensible lump sum every month and put any extra aside for emergencies. I'm in the middle of trying to do this myself and it's incredibly hard, but I know it will be worth it to get a proper handle on my spending!

7. PLAN FOR THE FUTURE

The biggest worry for most freelancers is related to income, so do some damage control by getting income protection insurance and setting aside money into a savings fund to cover quiet spells, cash-flow issues or sick pay. If you're based in the UK, please, please, please make sure you set up a pension to get your government top-up (you aren't auto-enrolled like those in regular employment). Definitely visit the government website of your own country to see if similar options are available and consider investing into a private pension too.

CHAPTER 13

ADMIN AND ORGANISATION

Let's play a fun game. Drink a shot of tequila every time you read the word 'spreadsheet'.

Seriously though, this chapter is going to seem – on the face of it – rather boring. But once you've implemented some of my advice (and downed three or four tequilas) life is going to be so much more rosy. Having basic systems in place to manage the admin side of freelancing takes a bit of work in the beginning and, admittedly, a few hours a month ongoing, but it will allow you the time and headspace to focus on the exciting parts of your business with much more clarity.

INVOICING

Creating and sending an invoice is actually way more simple than you might think. Yes, there are online services and software available that might make life easier once you need to send out lots and lots of invoices every month, but in the beginning you can do it all in a Word document. I use Pages, which has a handy invoice template that you can customise and start using immediately. You can add your own logo if you want to be fancy but it's not essential.

If you're in the UK, here's what you need to include in every invoice:[41]

- a unique identification number (see section on 'order numbers' on page 152 for more on this)
- your company name, address and contact information
- the company name and address of the customer you're invoicing
- a clear description of what you're charging for
- the date the goods or service were provided
- the date of the invoice
- the amount(s) being charged
- VAT amount if applicable
- the total amount owed

If you're a sole trader, the invoice must also include:

- your name and any business name being used
- an address where any legal documents can be delivered to you if you are using a business name

(As always, if you're outside the UK do check your own government guidelines.)

WHEN TO SEND AN INVOICE?

Well, it's kind of up to you, but ideally it should be stipulated beforehand in your contract. For clients on retainer (i.e. we've agreed that I will deliver the same type of work for them every month on a recurring basis), send your invoice on the last day of the month or the first day of the next month.

E.g. for work completed in October, send the invoice on 31st October or 1st November.

For one-off projects, you can send the invoice as soon as the client has received the work. Depending on the client, I'll sometimes wait for confirmation to make sure they're happy with the work (again, depending on the terms set out in the original contract) but generally the sooner you can send the invoice the better. People rarely pay promptly so get the ball rolling to minimise delays. For bigger jobs or ones that require a lot of back and forth between you and the client (e.g. website design, branding), it's advisable that you ask for half the money upfront. In my field of journalism that simply won't wash (it's often payment on publication, which can be months after the work is submitted), but I know that it's really common in other creative industries such as video production or photography. I'm considering trying it out with bigger content-writing projects. Therapists, for example, may choose to take the entire payment upon booking an appointment which seems totally normal to me from a customer's perspective. If you're worried about putting people off with this method, you can always start by taking a partial payment of 20%.

TIP: Be careful with wording in your contracts. Taking a 'deposit' can be misconstrued as a refundable fee. If this isn't the case, consider using the phrase 'partial payment' or 'payment plan' to make things clear.

ORDER NUMBERS

One thing that I didn't keep on top of in the beginning was my order numbers. Every invoice needs to be assigned a number (it's like waiting on your burger at Five Guys) so that you and your customer can track payments. Some companies will use any excuse to delay payment, so make sure that every invoice you send has all the correct information on it from the word go. The easiest way to do this manually is to simply create an invoices spreadsheet (*wahey, get that first tequila down the hatch!*) with a list of ascending numbers, and every time you need to raise an invoice, move down the list and add in the details of your invoice (e.g. date, customer name, amount owed) so that you can track them in the future if required. Which leads us nicely on to…

KEEPING TRACK OF PAYMENTS

If you're sending lots of invoices every month (which soon you will be, you legend), it's important to make sure that you actually receive payment. It's easier than you think to forget about that invoice you sent at 5 am the morning before you went on holiday, or to assume that a reliable client will keep up to date with every payment. One of my favourite clients missed a payment one month and it was just human error. Remember lots of your clients are just like you, trying to run a business with limited time and resources, so don't make the mistake of thinking that everyone has a finance department taking care of all their bills. Once you've created your invoice tracking spreadsheet (mentioned above), you can keep an eye on any payments outstanding. It's good to do this on a monthly basis – say, at the same time as you're doing your income spreadsheets. You'll be looking at your bank statements anyway, so you might as well check on what payments are due.

I like to use the Boomerang method. This is especially helpful if you send invoices at random times throughout the month, like me. In the UK, unless you agree a payment date, the customer must pay you within thirty days of getting your invoice or receiving the goods or service.[42] So if you send twenty invoices on different dates over a one-month period then it can understandably get a bit complicated trying to keep tabs on when payments are deemed late.

To help with this, I use a Gmail service called Boomerang, which allows you to set automated reminders when emails go unanswered. Whenever I email an invoice I set it to Boomerang thirty days later if I haven't had a response, which highlights the original email and bumps it to the top of my inbox. This automatically reminds me to check whether I've received payment or not. This technique isn't fool-proof (if your client sends you an email saying thanks for your invoice then it doesn't work), but it adds another layer to your invoicing system and can stop things falling through the cracks. It also takes approximately two seconds to implement, so it's worth giving a go.

TIP: Keep a Post-It note on your wall or computer screen with a list of payments due and score them off as they arrive. I find this helps calm my daily (and hourly) panic about having earnt enough money each month.

CONTRACTS

A contract is simply an agreement between two or more parties – in this case, between you and your client. The good news is that an exchange of emails can be legally binding (depending on the context), so don't worry if you don't have any contracts in place just yet. Just plan on making it a priority.

Websites such as Rocket Lawyer and Farillio allow you to purchase one-off documents or subscribe monthly to get access to multiple documents and advice from lawyers. Then, once you have a template that reflects your needs, you can change the details to suit any jobs that come up in the future. Every business is different, so I can't show you an example (in case you just copy and paste it and blame me when you're legally obliged to write them a bestselling thriller novel when you were only supposed to be designing a logo), but generally it should include:

- Parties involved (i.e. you and the client)
- Date
- The type of work to be carried out
- What your service will provide
- What you will not provide
- Delivery terms
- Payment terms
- Space for both parties to sign and date

EMAILS

Why is everyone so obsessed with inbox zero? I never delete emails, because you never know when you'll need to refer to a random conversation you had with a client six months ago.

It happens, seriously. Obviously you don't want to be *that* guy ('as per your previous email' is a phrase that should be used rarely, if at all), but if a client contradicts themselves or says you've not delivered what you promised, having an electronic paper trail will help you stand your ground. Just bear in mind that the same goes for anything *you've* said in emails...

ORGANISING YOUR INBOX

Even though I don't delete emails, I do tend to file away ones that I know I'll need in the future. There are quite a few different ways you can label and organise emails, but the most basic way to make a start is to have a separate folder for each client you work with and store all communications in the corresponding files. If you work with one client on multiple projects you could then create sub-categories to keep everything separate. You might also benefit from folders dedicated to other areas of your business such as client feedback, potential clients, tax returns and expense receipts.

If you're overwhelmed with the number of emails you get in general, deal with urgent emails in the morning and file anything else that needs actioned in a folder called 'not-urgent', then set aside thirty minutes at the end of the day to tackle what you can. Once the thirty minutes is up, you're done. Anything that isn't dealt with can wait until the next afternoon because – you've guessed it – it's not urgent.

HELPFUL DOCUMENTS

As you get busier, you'll probably find you spend a lot of time doing the same things over and over again. This is when it's helpful to have a collection of documents that act as canned responses to give people the information they need without you having to type out a massive email every single time. Here are a few examples:

RATES SHEET

One email query I get a lot is about guest posts on my blog. While I'm not averse to the odd guest post if it truly adds value (and isn't selling something totally random like a lawnmower), I just don't have the time to go through every pricing option. The truth is most people who enquire aren't actually willing to pay to be featured on my blog, so taking the time to craft a detailed response is often a total waste of time. This is why I created a rates sheet. It details my blogging services very clearly, including prices. This means when I get the inevitable 'Hello Fionalikestoblog.com' (bad start to an email BTW, just sayin'), I'm armed and ready to reply with a ready-to-go two-page document that will either put people off, or start a dialogue with potential clients.

MEDIA KIT

If you're a blogger, then you'll benefit from this and maybe even already have one. It's a simple document summarising your services as well as your statistics (e.g. page views, Instagram followers, email subscribers) to potential clients. Most incorporate images and are branded to tie in with your blog style.

TIP: Get a free account with Canva. It's a super simple graphic design tool with thousands of readymade templates that will make your documents look professional.

FAQ SECTION

If you get a lot of enquiries then you can save heaps of time by adding a Frequently Asked Questions page to your website. This can work well if you are constantly asked about the same things, such as how to apply to be on your podcast or how your booking process works. People won't necessarily read it before they contact you, but it's much quicker to send a link to a detailed answer as opposed to typing out the same information again and again.

SOME HANDY ADMIN AND ORGANISATION TOOLS

Monday.com: An online platform that allows you to set out tasks visually. If you collaborate with others you can assign them tasks, leave comments and update each task as it progresses from start to finish. Really satisfying if you like visual tools and seeing long lists of all the tasks you've completed. Other popular task-management apps include Trello and Asana.

Google Docs: Share, edit and add comments to documents. Great for collaboration. Has helpful tools for creating snazzy-looking booklets and slideshows.

Google Drive: Share images, spreadsheets, videos and other files without them getting lost in email threads.

Google Keep: Note-taking app for your phone with cool features such as the ability to scan documents, save

I feel like I've got my sh*t together when I use my diary.

images, links, add voice notes and organise with labels. You can set location reminders so that when you are in a certain area you get a notification. Great if you're always forgetting to pick up fabric softener.

Google Forms: A handy way to gather information from new clients (e.g. design brief, contact details) as well as collecting testimonials and feedback.

DEAR DIARY

I love my diary. It makes me feel organised. Like, 'I can see the bottom of my laundry basket' organised. Like the way I imagine Kim Kardashian might feel after she's had her closet professionally arranged. You get the idea: I feel like I've got my sh*t together when I use my diary.

I write everything about my work schedule in it, as well as dinner dates, coffee with friends, doctor's appointments and my Sunday yoga session. When I open it up and find today's date, I feel focused. As I write this, it sits next to me on my desk, patiently waiting for me whenever I need it. I bought it online, had it imported from America and it cost me over £40, which is pretty steep considering it will only last twelve months. But I can say hand on heart that I would pay double, maybe even triple, that amount for a diary that makes me feel this way (no, *you're* being dramatic) because it's had such a huge impact on my organisation levels.

Having a diary system that you're happy with will change your life, but finding one that works for you might take a bit of trial and error. I like to write my to-do lists in my diary (they get lost otherwise), so I make sure there's blank space for that. I also like practising some loose time-blocking (purposefully assigning blocks of time to specific tasks), so having time slots in the margin of each day really helps. I don't work day to day; I work week to week, meaning that I need a week-view diary so that I can see clearly what the next seven days have in store. I keep a keen eye on my mental health and like to plan in downtime after stressful events like public speaking or meetings in London. If I can see my week at a glance, I can plan more effectively.

Colour-coding is fun (I use highlighters to draw my attention to deadlines and meetings) although obviously not essential. I take great pleasure in planning out the next seven days on a Friday afternoon, normally with an extra-large mocha in hand and my favourite true crime podcast playing through my headphones. I tried planning on a Sunday evening, but my head just isn't in gear then. By that time the weekend has chilled me right out and I'm not feeling worky. On a Friday I feel accomplished and motivated, so that's when I plan.

Paper diaries give some people the heebie jeebies. I get that. Digital diaries are great because you can sync your calendar with colleagues, which is ideal if you work in a team or outsource to other freelancers. You could even sync up your calendar with clients if you have regular meetings. You can't lose a digital diary (unless you lose your phone, but most apps will have a desktop version you can log into at any time). If you're always forgetting appointments then you can set up notifications for important events and you'll never forget anyone's birthday again. Depending on the app it's also free and, I suppose, better for the environment depending on which paper diary you choose. Okay, I can see the upside of a digital diary now, but still, I love a paper diary.

(Is this book becoming about how much I love my diary? Well, this is awkward.)

MONTH-END ADMIN LIST

Everybody has their own system for handling the boring admin that comes with freelancing. I personally cannot face the thought of having to catch up on a year's worth of paperwork when it comes to doing my tax return, so I keep on top of everything on a monthly basis. Here's a brief rundown of how I do that without too much hassle.

RECEIPTS
Keep all receipts in relation to anything you spend on the business (refer back to Chapter 9 for more details). For paper receipts you can either keep them on file or scan/photograph them and store them digitally. There are some apps (e.g. Expensify) that allow you to do this too. Anything that you buy online should come with an email confirmation and a receipt. You can store these on your email account in a separate folder with a catchy name. I suggest something simple like 'expenses'.

INVOICES
As I mentioned earlier, start a spreadsheet that keeps track of all your invoice numbers and amounts charged.

(God, this chapter is dull, isn't it? But you should power through as it's probably still slightly better than sitting in an office doing a job you hate.)

INCOME

Create a simple spreadsheet and start to document your income from the very beginning. Trust me, it makes doing your tax return so much quicker. I find the easiest way to do this is at the end of each month. I go through print-offs of my bank statement and highlight any payments in, and then add this information to a simple table which adds up the total. Make sure you add in all the information related to the payment (invoice number, client name, service provided) so that you can track them in the future.

EXPENSES

Using the receipts that you've been diligently collecting all month, create a spreadsheet and input all the information (e.g. Hotel: £150) and create a total. Again, I highly recommend (nay, *demand*) you do this on a monthly basis so that at the end of the tax year you have waaaaay less admin to take care of.

You can do all of what I've just mentioned with accounting software such as QuickBooks or Xero and loads of people swear by it. Personally, though, I find ye olde spreadsheet system works just fine.

CHECKLIST

- Create an invoice template
- Create a spreadsheet to document all information associated with every invoice you send
- Download a contract template

- Organise your inbox
- Find a diary that works for you
- Get your monthly admin routine sorted
- Take another shot of tequila for good luck

CHAPTER 14

WHEN SH*T HITS THE FAN

For every life-changing moment that comes with the OOO
life, there is an equally dramatic moment which feels quite
the opposite. The kind of moment that makes you shake
your fist at the sky, send fifteen WhatsApp messages to your
best mate in ALL CAPS or have a good long ugly cry in the
shower. In life, nothing ever pans out the way you think. In
business, it's even more prevalent. As much as you like to
think that you can predict what's coming next, at some point
you need to plan for the unplannable. You need to be ready
when sh*t hits the fan.

Here are some not-so-fun things that every freelancer
should expect:

AN EMPTY BANK ACCOUNT

Yup, this is up there as the number one concern for every
freelancer I know. Quite often an empty bank account is only
temporary as you wait to be paid for work you've done in the
past. This is when having a buffer fund can really save your
bacon, as you can eat into your savings for a few weeks until
payments clear. (Just remember to try to pay it back into
your savings.)

There's also no shame in signing up with an agency to do some ad hoc work like waiting tables, serving drinks at events or doing some virtual assistant work. We've all been there. My friend spent one summer working at festivals mostly to see bands play for free, but she also made some money at the same time.

If you need money ASAP, then here are some epic tips taken from the @go _fund_yourself_ Instagram page:

- If you have a decent camera you can sell pictures on Shutterstock, Flickr, Alamy and iStock
- Help out with Airbnb changeovers and greet guests (use Facebook and Nextdoor.com to advertise)
- Upsell furniture then resell on Etsy
- Sell clothes on Depop
- Rent out your equipment (cameras, drones, musical instruments, etc.) via Fat Llama
- Rent out your bike via Spinlister
- Sell unused items on Gumtree or Facebook Marketplace
- Rent out your parking space with YourParkingSpace or ParkAtMyHouse

THE CLIENT FROM HELL

If you think having a sh*tty boss ruins your working week, then wait until you have a sh*tty client. Jumping through hoops for someone who you don't mesh well with is exhausting, but basically a job requirement if you want paid-for work. Sh*tty clients can come in a number of guises, including:

MISSING MAISY

This is the one who goes AWOL for days or maybe even weeks. Normally this happens towards the end of a project and you're waiting on them to sign off on the work you've completed. Sometimes they go missing as soon as the invoice has been sent. Maisy is a tricky one. Sometimes she genuinely is busy, other times she's acting the goat. My advice would be to give her the benefit of the doubt for thirty days but chase her up with a friendly email every week. If she's overdue on payment then send a new invoice with late payment fees attached. (See page 168 for more details on late fees.)

STARRY-EYED SARAH

This open-hearted soul believes that you can change the world. She is optimistic. Too optimistic. She expects you to go above and beyond what you agreed on in your initial meeting, is constantly adding to your workload, asking for last-minute favours and not paying the price. You need to be strict. Refer back to your contract and be clear on what you will and won't provide. Suggest an hourly fee for any extra tasks she assigns you and be wary of answering emails outside of your normal working hours.

BROKEBACK MOUNTAIN

Sometimes you have to be the one to say goodbye, even though it feels awkward and goes against every natural instinct. Turning away work just feels wrong. But it's not. I've worked with clients who I knew weren't the right fit for months while internally screaming, 'I wish I knew how to quit you' without a clue how to end the arrangement.

Sometimes I got lucky, and they ended things first. Here are a few phrases that work:

- I think that your needs would be better served by someone who specialises in _____
- Due to changes in my business I will be unable to work on your account as of [insert date]
- I regret to inform you that I'll no longer be able to provide any further services, but can happily recommend [name] to pick up where I left off

LATE PAYMENTS

Xero statistics show that small businesses are owed an average of £23,360 in overdue invoices on any one day and have to wait fourteen days after the due date to be paid.[43] The most commonly accepted system for paying invoices is a bank transfer within thirty days, but 42% of business-owners agree that this model is outdated.

You should agree beforehand on a payment date. After this date, payments are late and you can claim interest and debt-recovery costs. Even if you don't agree on a payment date, in the UK the law states that payment is late if it has not arrived thirty days after either:

- the customer gets the invoice
- you deliver the goods or provide the service (if this is later)[44]

(If you're outside of the UK, make sure to check your country's own laws on late payments.)

Most freelancers don't have the money to get lawyers involved in chasing up late payments. The issue of unpaid invoices is something that almost every freelancer is painfully aware of, but without legal backing many struggle to get the money they are owed. Here are my tips on dealing with unpaid invoices:

- Make your payment terms clear from the outset
- Send invoices at regular intervals, especially for big projects
- As soon as an invoice becomes late, cease any further work until it's resolved
- Get insurance that covers you for legal costs or offers a service that chases up late payments

TIP: Offer clients a discount if they pay in advance.

YOU'VE MISSED A DEADLINE

Imagine sitting down to check your emails, fresh morning cuppa in hand, only to find out that you were supposed to deliver a piece of work the day before. And you haven't even made a start on it. Somehow it slipped your mind completely. In this situation, honesty is always the best policy. Hold your hands up and admit you did wrong, instead of making thinly veiled excuses while you try to cobble something together in a few hours. If you hand in sloppy work it will only have a negative impact on your long-term relationship with this client, so be upfront. Pick up the phone (an email won't cut it here I'm afraid) and beg for forgiveness and, of course, an extension on the deadline. Don't forget to forgive yourself. The chances are no one died as a result of your error and it's a learning experience that you'll definitely learn from.

YOU'VE GOT NO WORK COMING IN

Dealing with a quiet spell (aka tumbleweed territory) is tough. You can lean into these periods if you're financially stable, i.e. take advantage of early-morning cinema screenings and start drinking gin in the afternoons while saying 'it's five o'clock somewhere'.

Once you've got bored of that, however, use the time to brush up on your knowledge. Learn some skills that will allow you to charge more or tap into new audiences, read those self-help books you've had stacked up on your bedside table, or start working on your novel. Ask past clients for feedback and analyse the results. Then use this lull as an opportunity to make adjustments to your packages and customer service based on your findings.

There's no denying that tumbleweed territory is scary. No money coming in isn't ideal, so here are some ways that you can prepare for (and potentially avoid) periods of drought:

SET UP A REFERRALS SCHEME

Offer existing clients a discount if they successfully refer you to someone who ends up paying for your services.

PUT CLIENTS ON A WAITING LIST

Once your books are full (I swear, it's a state of being that truly exists), invite future clients to go on a waiting list. This means that you plan to slot them into your schedule as soon as you have an opening. If you can, nurture this email list by sending out free content too.

HAVE MULTIPLE INCOME STREAMS

It's cool to specialise in one area of expertise, but don't shoot yourself in the foot. I'm an author, but I don't make all my money writing books. I write press releases, blog posts, eBooks and Facebook posts as well as many other things. (Refer back to Chapter 10 to learn more about how to diversify your own income streams.)

LOOK FOR IN-HOUSE WORK

One great thing about freelancing is that it puts you in a position to take on temporary or part-time contracts that most people don't want. Keep your eye out for part-time work or maternity leave cover on job sites, or sign up to receive notifications by email. I know that looking for a job might feel like you're moving backwards, but if you find a role doing the work you love, then it's still progress. Working in-house can also offer a unique chance to make some stellar industry connections that you might be able to call on for freelance work in the future. You'll probably brush up on some of your lesser-used skills as well.

YOU KEEP HITTING A BRICK WALL

Get comfortable with hearing the word 'no'. In freelancing there are a lot of positive conversations, upbeat emails and high-energy networking events that promise lucrative

Be ready to let rejections bounce off you, otherwise they'll knock you down entirely.

work. Work that never comes to fruition. I'm not saying be pessimistic, but you need to be ready to let rejections bounce off you, otherwise they'll knock you down entirely. Try reframing failure like this:

- Each failure is just one of hundreds and thousands of events that happen as part of your business. One small failure doesn't make you a failure as a person.
- A loss does not negate all your wins.
- The important lesson from failure doesn't come from falling down; it comes from getting back up. When you're ready, try again with gusto.
- Failure is proof of persistence, and persistence leads to success.
- Be brave. John Wayne once said, 'Courage is being scared to death but saddling up anyway.'

YOU'VE TAKEN ON TOO MUCH

List all the work you have on and write a pros and cons list of each project. Maybe some pay well but the work is really boring. No doubt others will be creatively stimulating but pay very little. Look at your finances. Can you afford to be working for peanuts even if the work is enjoyable? Can you delay some of the work you're doing? Being honest is always easier than you think, and people can be flexible with deadlines, but only if you actually ask!

LOSING A CLIENT

I lost a major client in the first year of freelancing. I was going to be about £700 short every month without this work coming in, so I panicked from the word go. It was a controlled panic, though. For five long minutes, I contemplated going back to work in a café. I imagined the early mornings, the coffee-stained jeans, the smell of dishwasher steam. It was a hard NOPE from me, so I put my thinking cap on. I called everyone I knew who could possibly need my services, chased up on old leads and found new ones. I joined every Facebook group for journalists and sent pitches to editors I had never worked with before. I found a function room in a local bar that was free to hire and started running ticketed events. I looked on job sites and found a part-time copywriting role. That summer I ended up earning a good chunk of money from multiple sources that I conjured out of thin air because of my initial loss. It wasn't luck; it was my mindset that made it happen. I decided that I was going to find a way to make up my income and I did.

As bestselling author Danielle LaPorte wisely said, 'The surest sign that you're working with the life-affirming kind of discipline, rather than the spirit-depressing kind, is that you don't complain very much about doing what it takes.'

TECHNICAL PROBLEMS

There's a common misconception that running your own business requires you to be a technical whizz. I spend upwards of 40 hours a week working on my laptop and I still need to google how to take a screen grab at least once a month. It's OK to get by with the basics, but there comes a time when we all need to call in the professionals. Here are a few tips on the subject:

GET SUPPORT

First of all, get a tech person on your side. It doesn't need to be someone you pay on a monthly retainer, but have a go-to person for all your tech queries. This is especially important if you run a business that depends on your website functioning at all times. An e-commerce store, for example, needs to be online to allow people to purchase products. Online courses and digital products are the same. If you're running a membership site then this is even more important because if your site goes down you'll lose sales and gain a bunch of disgruntled users in the process. Talk to other freelancers in your field and find out who they use. Recommendations are always a good idea, and the good thing with technical support is that they don't need to work locally to help you out as most tasks can be done remotely.

BACK IT UP

Laptop issues? Please tell me you backed everything up? I have no technical knowledge, but personally I use a Cloud service (e.g. Dropbox, Google Drive, Microsoft OneDrive) so that everything backs up automatically without me ever needing to worry. My advice? Back it all up. Now. I'll wait.

TIP: Keep family and work computers separate to make sure you can always work without causing any arguments. This will also stop any issues when work is accidentally deleted and ensures you are keeping client details confidential.

TIP: Buy spare chargers for your laptop and phone and keep them in the bag you use when you're out of the house. This means you don't need to remember to pack them every time you have to work on the go.

CHECKLIST

- Think about diversifying your income
- Be prepared to deal with tricky clients
- Put a system in place for late payments
- Get comfortable with things not going to plan
- Seek technical backup

PART THREE

MAKING THE SHOW SUSTAINABLE

Almost everyone I've spoken to as part of the research for this book has admitted that in the early days of freelancing, they didn't have a clue what they were doing. Some forgot to pay their tax bill. Others worked sixteen-hour days for months on end. Many made a dog's dinner of the first year of self-employment, yet they stuck with it and managed to succeed.

When I ditched my part-time café job and tried freelancing full-time, I didn't announce it on social media. I told my friends and family and quietly got on with things because it honestly felt like a bit of an experiment. It felt scary to be responsible for finding ways to make money every month and so I told myself in those first few months that, worst-case scenario, I could always go back to working in a café.

After a year of living OOO, however, I knew that I really didn't want to give it up. That's when I realised that this experiment had turned into a fully fledged career choice and that I would have to up the ante if I wanted it to become a sustainable way of life.

In the beginning, I made a lot of mistakes. Don't get me wrong, I think mistakes are normal (i.e. attempting to cut one's own fringe), but it's important that we learn from them and grow (luckily a dodgy fringe grows out pretty quickly).

Getting paid is only part of the process. There is so much more that goes into running a business, from building your own community and networking with other freelancers to learning how to sell and giving excellent customer service. Once you've opened the door into the world of freelancing, you quickly realise that there are a million different paths you can follow, so many things that need to be done and so many ways to make it work. This section of the book aims to scratch the surface of what it takes to thrive as a freelancer as opposed to merely survive. From productivity to putting up your rates, the next few chapters offer a range of ideas to make the most of your time and help your business go from strength to strength.

CHAPTER 15

FINDING YOUR PEOPLE

Working from home can be a lonely old business, but that's why many of us like it in the first place. I love my own company and, quite honestly, feel drained if I have to spend more than a few hours working in a group setting. But working alone constantly isn't healthy for our minds or our careers. I know it might seem counterintuitive to start socialising as part of your business (especially if you're an introvert like me), but I urge you to read this section with an open mind and try to imagine the wider impact it could have on your business growth.

DEALING WITH SOLITUDE

I spoke earlier in the book about why having the flexibility to work from home can be beneficial. One report published by jobsite Indeed found that 75% of employees who are allowed to work from home say that doing so has improved their work-life balance. Those surveyed also reported reduced stress levels, absences and sick days, as well as improved morale.[45]

However, research into those who are self-employed shows that remote working can have a negative impact too. One report published by IPSE in partnership with PeoplePerHour says,

> *The need for more regular client feedback and feelings of loneliness were especially prominent among millennials, with almost a third saying they felt lonely because of remote working. This suggests many of them are yet to build up their confidence or adopt techniques to help them connect with people.*[46]

Basically, working from home is great for getting sh*t done, but it might not necessarily make you happy all the time. After more than ten years of working in teams, I was overjoyed to set up a business in my front room. I definitely felt more balanced, relaxed and in control of my moods. But after a year or so I started to realise that I wasn't always flourishing in my solitude. There were days when I didn't hear the sound of my own voice until my husband returned home at 6 pm. There were afternoons when I needed to move my body so desperately that I created a sad, solo mosh pit in my bedroom with the help of Guns N' Roses. And as much as I tried to feel grateful for my flexible lifestyle, I just wanted to talk to another freelancer and quietly whisper, 'This is a bit sh*t sometimes, isn't it?'

THE IMPORTANCE OF RELATIONSHIPS

I'm not making this up by the way. Research shows that social relationships affect mental health, health behaviour, physical health and mortality risk.[47] Business Insider reported that 'regardless of your heart health, social isolation can increase risk of death anywhere from 50–90%. Being socially disconnected can also up your risk of developing high blood pressure or inflammation, and make people more aggressive.'

I'm especially interested in the psychological impact, because being in the right mindset when you're OOO can make or break your business.

Connecting with other humans is said to offer a form of 'social support' that can reduce the impact of stress, give you a sense of meaning as well as the feeling of being loved, cared for and heard. It can also enhance your sense of personal control, giving you the belief that you can take actions that lead to positive outcomes.[48]

Some studies talk about the 'symbolic meaning' of social ties, something that I think is definitely on the rise in the freelancing world. Relationships such as marriage come with meanings attached. To have and to hold. Till death do us part. Having meaningful interactions with fellow freelancers is just as important. In the same way that members of a football team work together on the basis that they all want the same thing, being part of a community of freelancers can give you the accountability, drive and confidence to push forward with your business. As Aaron Antonovsky writes in *Unraveling the Mystery of Health: How People Manage Stress and Stay Well*: 'In a more fundamental way, greater social connection may foster a sense of 'coherence' or meaning and purpose in life, which, in turn, enhances mental health, physiological processes, and physical health.'[49]

The most important part of socialising for me is the ability to bounce my ideas off others. Yes, I could ask my husband or the postman (literally the only two people I meet sometimes if I don't make the effort to engage socially), but they don't necessarily 'get' it. They don't live in my world of running a creative business, so often it's much more beneficial for me to talk to other women who are in the same boat as me. In an article published on the Fast Company website, author Jeff Goins writes about the importance of communities for creatives:

'Without a community, our best work will stay stuck inside us. We need peer groups and circles of influence to make our work *better*. This is true in art, but it's also true in business. Any work that requires you to make something the world hasn't seen before is work that often has to be done collaboratively.'[50]

Other notable benefits of building relationships as a freelancer include:

- The ability to sound off about things that only other freelancers understand
- Getting advice on how to navigate awkward client situations
- Learning from other people's experience
- Shared expertise from other industries
- Skill-swapping opportunities
- Recommending each other's services to new clients
- Sharing costs of online courses, equipment or office space

I love nothing more than hiding myself away from the world and getting on with work, especially when I'm on a tight deadline. But be wary. Alone time might be good for output and productivity, but if it's starting to affect your mind, then not only are you doing a disservice to your health, you're doing a disservice to your business too.

HOW TO MAKE FRIENDS

- Get a dog, you'll know everyone in your area within a week
- Check local notice boards for book clubs, yoga classes, etc

- Search MeetUp
- Join an online membership site
- Chat in your local Facebook community group
- Offer a skill-swap

In between my lonely dance parties I realised that human connection was probably going to be a non-negotiable part of my week, and so I tried lots of different ways to interact with others, slowly building up my own network of people to lean on. I may not have an office space to work in, but I like to think that I have a few virtual colleagues who are always around if I need to chat. What follows comes as a result of my quest to find freelancing friends and break away from the solitude of working home alone...

ONLINE COMMUNITIES

The internet is like a giant hotel lobby at a freelancer conference. Everyone is just hanging out, sharing stories and ready to chat. Freelance Heroes, The Freelance Lifestylers and the Being Freelance Community are my current fave Facebook groups, and they've helped me with those moments when I just need to rant about something miniscule like a glitch in some image editing software or how I burnt my toast this morning. Basically, I use them in the same way as you would a water cooler in the office: as a place to gossip, reflect and blow off some steam.

There are also some awesome paid-for communities that can connect you with other freelancers who are looking for moral support:

- **Grow & Glow**, a membership site created by blogger Vix Meldrew, is for creators who want to build an audience and get sponsorships but need expert training to make it happen.
- **UnderPinned** is an online platform with an app designed to help freelancers manage projects, find work and get paid on time. It also has an online magazine and hosts regular events in London.
- **The Independent Girls Collective**, a membership site run by accountant Julia Day, helps women grow their businesses through online courses and coaching.

These are just a few of the online communities that I've observed recently and I know that there are more cropping up every day as freelancers continue to grow in numbers.

I've found The Independent Girls Collective to be particularly positive for me because I have a lot in common with the founder, Julia. We both talk quite openly about mental health and love reading business books. I also had a business coaching session with her and that really helped me take control of things at a point when I was feeling overwhelmed with growing an online presence while writing this book. I asked her to give a broader view of some of the positive connections that she's witnessed as part of her online membership site, and she told me that 'a few members of mine have become real-life friends and set up co-working, found clients in the community and even set up businesses together.'

As well as using it as a space to socialise, members have essentially co-opted the platform as a sort of peer-to-peer learning service. As Julia explains, 'It's a place to ask questions that they can't ask elsewhere. There's normally someone in the group who can give advice or context on things like how much to charge or get education on things they don't know about. Sharing experiences is a huge thing.'

I've been harping on about the power of online communities since 2016(ish). I'd been blogging about my experience with mental illness for a few years and the penny finally dropped when I kept receiving emails and comments from strangers who told me about their own struggles. Together in our shared experiences we felt emotionally validated knowing that others truly understood what we had been going through.

One thing I felt intensely when I was first diagnosed with depression was isolation. I didn't work for a long time so I stayed home alone. I soon developed anxiety and this prevented me from going out, so I became even more withdrawn. Although not every freelancer works alone, a notable number of UK freelancers say that they experience feelings of loneliness and isolation,[51] and there is some emerging research that shows online communities can tackle this problem.

One such study suggests that participants who experienced 'considerable social and geographical isolation' used online forums which provided 'a *social connection* that was lacking in their everyday lives'.[52] Although this study concerns people with mental illness and those who care for people with mental illness, it shows the powerful link between online connections and real-life benefits.

TIP: If you can't find an online community that feels right, or you want to target a niche industry or interest, set up your own. It's free to set up a Facebook group, or you can use other services like Slack. What are you waiting for?

Once you start connecting with other freelancers online, you'll be surprised how many there are.

According to Vix Meldrew, online communities, having a network of people who are essentially acting as your colleagues, can be really valuable:

I think that in a creative industry it's quite an insular thing. Freelancers tend to put a lot of their self-worth in what they do. By giving someone else their platform or saying, 'Go to this person because they're an expert', it's almost like they think people will think that they themselves are rubbish. But that's an internal feeling. That used to be me. I didn't want to ask for help. I wanted to know it all, be the best and never get anything wrong because I thought that was the only way to get people to trust in me, but since doing Grow & Glow I've realised I can't talk about every topic. I need to enlist experts like Pinterest and TikTok, but also individual freelancers too. It's good for me and it's good for them too.

CO-WORKING

Once you start connecting with other freelancers online, you'll be surprised how many there are. We truly are everywhere, just lurking around, quietly tapping in the corner of almost every Starbucks across the land. So, once you've dipped your toe into an online community, ask if there is anyone in your area that would like to go for a coffee. If you're not brave enough for that just yet, search within the Facebook groups you've found to see if there are any regular meet-ups. If not, why not suggest one and get a few people together for co-working? You can also search for local get-togethers on event sites such as MeetUp and Eventbrite. Don't forget to check your local newspaper too.

I spoke to Jessica Berry, who is based in Nottingham, UK. She was struggling with the loneliness of freelancing and wanted to connect with women in a similar position, so she set up The Co-Working Club. They meet once a week, normally in a café with lots of coffee and cake, and get to work on whatever they want surrounded by people, just like a traditional office environment.

'It would probably sound cheesy to say that The Co-Working Club has changed my life,' Jessica told me, 'but in so many ways it has.' Not only does the meet-up give her a structure to her week, but it also provides motivation and a sense of community – something that so many freelancers miss out on by working home alone.

Being around a group of creative and inspiring women fuels me up to experiment more within my own business, helps me to push through the difficult times as well as celebrate the achievements. Sometimes freelancing can make you feel incredibly alone, but with The Co-Working Club by my side I feel like I have a community of cheerleaders supporting me every step of the way!

Co-working doesn't need to be you in a public space with ten or twenty other people. The flexibility of freelancing should suit your needs, so if you'd rather work with fewer people then that's cool. Or maybe you find it too distracting and instead decide to have your lunch break with a fellow freelancer so that you can socialise together instead of work together. Author Poorna Bell admitted to me recently that the typical co-working environment doesn't float her boat.

'I find them really noisy,' she says. 'I thought that I was a bad freelancer because everyone else seems to love that environment and I find it hard work. I think there are different ways you can connect with others. You don't have to do what everyone else is doing. I mean, yeah, we're all freelancers, but what works for someone won't work for everyone.'

TIP: If you don't like the idea of working in a group setting, make a regularly recurring work date with one freelancer you really get on with and stick to it.

DREADED NETWORKING EVENTS

As I've mentioned previously, I was diagnosed with anxiety after a mental breakdown in my mid-twenties, and it soon became obvious to me that this was triggered by social situations. Busy pubs made my heart race, my palms sweat. I would hide in even the smelliest of bathrooms to find a moment of calm. Even seemingly harmless interactions like family meals made me feel vulnerable. Socialising was the hardest thing for me to do, and it took years for me to learn to be comfortable in those situations.

Now, I can enter a room of strangers and make eye contact easily. I don't own the room – that's just not my personality style – but I can approach people and start a conversation. One of the most awkward social situations you'll ever be faced with as a freelancer is a networking event. It's a room full of people who are eager to promote themselves, so the whole thing can feel a bit fake.

But they can result in you getting more clients, or maybe even a friend. At the very least, you'll have fulfilled your obligation to mingle with the rest of the human race and, as we already know, that will only do good things for your body and mind.

TOP TIPS FOR SURVIVING THE STRANGE PHENOMENON THAT IS A NETWORKING EVENT

- Wear something snazzy. It gives people something to compliment you on.
- Take business cards and give them to anyone you have a nice conversation with. Don't give them to arseholes.
- To get out of a boring conversation, say, 'I'm so sorry to interrupt but I've just spotted someone I promised I would say hello to.'
- Imagine how you'll feel after the event is over and focus on that positive outcome instead of the nerves you may be currently experiencing.
- Don't get drunk.
- Acknowledge how weird networking is, find someone in the room who looks nervous and say to them, 'I always find these events so nerve-wracking.' They'll instantly love you.
- Embrace your fear. Kirsty Hulse, brain-based coach and founder of Roar Training, says that we can harness modest levels of anxiety to our advantage: 'It's all about finding that sweet spot of letting the nerves be there but not letting them take over. And if you feel like they are about to take over, do something to lower your cortisol

levels like talking to a friend, laughing, feeling socially supported and reframe the situation as an opportunity for reward.'

NOTE: There is a difference between feeling nervous about networking and having crippling anxiety. If you're physically trembling or having panic attacks, then it's probably a good idea to get that under control first (with the help of a GP and/or therapist) before you push yourself into attending networking events.

CHECKLIST

- Find local freelancers in your area
- Join online communities
- Try co-working with other freelancers
- Give networking a go

CHAPTER 16

SELLING YOURSELF

In the beginning, you might get lucky with your first few clients. They might even fall right into your lap. They might come through a chance meeting at an event, a friend, or a relative of someone who you start chatting to on social media. But as your skill set grows and you get an appetite for the OOO life, you'll realise that you need a steady flow of customers. So, whether you are selling eBooks or delivering coaching sessions, teaching sewing or Spanish, you need to get comfortable with selling yourself.

WHAT IS MARKETING?

I struggle to answer this question as there are so many aspects of selling that come under the 'marketing' umbrella, but the umbrella itself is probably much bigger than you think. In her book *Simple Tips Smart Ideas: Build a Bigger Better Business*, Erica Wolfe-Murray says,

> *Marketing can be as simple or as in-depth as you want. It is about reminding your existing customers of what you do, and telling potential customers about your products/services to encourage*

them to buy from or work with you. And it's a mixture of art and science.

In her book, she also explains the difference between your audience and your target market. I found this part super helpful, because it allows you to see the importance of communication to people who you know are never going to be the ones to pay for your products or services. This is because your audience is anyone you want to think a certain way about your brand. It's the mum who will be paying for a teenager's maths tutor, the husband who will be shopping for birthday gifts, the journalist who will be publishing a review of your book or the social media manager who will be tagging you on their Twitter feed. Your target market, on the other hand, is the group of people you're aiming to sell to directly. This could still be the mum or the husband, but it's also the end user.

It's important to have a clear idea of who your audience and target market is so that you can tailor your marketing efforts to suit them. For example, take the mum looking for a maths tutor. What papers does she read? What social media platforms is she checking regularly? Where does she socialise? You can then use this information to perhaps place an advertisement in the local newspaper, school newsletter or post on the community Facebook group. Maybe you could put up posters in the local yoga studios and supermarkets.

WHAT IS PR?

Public relations is all about increasing awareness of your brand, typically through media such as podcasts, magazines, social media and television. Most experts agree that PR is a key part of a wider marketing strategy, so I won't go into too much depth about PR itself, although some of the marketing advice mentioned should result in good PR for your business. For an in-depth guide on how to manage your own PR, read *Hype Yourself: A No-Nonsense PR Toolkit For Small Businesses* by Lucy Werner. It's got lots of simple advice on how to set up your own press office and start implementing your own strategy. After reading the first few chapters I successfully pinned down my target audience and the value that I deliver as a freelancer – something that I hadn't previously written down on paper. It helped me get very specific with my digital marketing and helped me land three of my dream clients!

CAN'T SELL, WON'T SELL

For some reason the idea of becoming a salesperson feels gross to me, as I'm sure it does to many of you. Maybe it's because so many of us have fallen victim to effective sales people in our personal lives and have been left feeling duped and out of pocket. I know I can't visit my local Lush store without one of the over-enthusiastic, pink-haired employees winning me over with a not-so-subtle 'I love that dress you're wearing!' before working their magic on me. I always end up leaving with a paper bag stuffed full with glittery soaps and bath bombs that I didn't intend on buying.

Maybe it's because we feel like we have no right to toot our own horns in the first place? I mean, it's one thing getting a few clients through word of mouth, but when it comes to actually marketing yourself online and in real life, it can feel like you're drowning in a sea of competitors who are doing everything much better than you. Comparing yourself to others and feeling like an imposter (see Chapter 4 for more on this) can be common occurrences for most freelancers, and they can both give you major self-doubt when you're trying to big yourself up to potential clients. In my own experience, feeling like a fraud can quickly escalate to intense feelings of hatred for my work as well as myself as a person. Combine imposter syndrome with the isolation of freelancing and I can spiral pretty quickly from a wobble to a full-blown meltdown. It's safe to say that this state of mind isn't conducive for effective self-promotion.

TIP: Every time you get some positive feedback from a client, print it off and put it on the wall in the space where you work. It will subliminally remind you that you are awesome at your job!

CHANGING YOUR MINDSET

Having the practical skills to sell yourself is one thing, but if you really can't believe that you're destined for great things, then you'll never improve. Research shows that your perspective on learning can have a tangible impact on how you develop over time.

American psychologist Dr Carol Dweck discovered the beliefs we hold around intelligence are linked to our achievements. With a 'fixed mindset', people believe that their basic abilities, intelligence and talents are just that: fixed. They don't think they can gain any more than they already have. Alternatively, in a 'growth mindset', people believe that their talents and abilities can be developed through effort, good teaching and persistence. They think everyone can get smarter if they work at it.[53]

I bring this up because it can be easy to brush off selling as something that you're innately good or bad at doing. If you adopt a 'growth mindset', however, you can learn to promote yourself in a way that not only feels right, but actually works.

BELIEVE IN WHAT YOU'RE SELLING

Working in a sandwich shop taught me a lot about why you need to love what you sell. When my boss wanted to introduce a vegan option, he settled on falafel. We all tried it and agreed it was delicious. When customers didn't know what kind of sandwich they wanted, we all recommended they try the falafel. Why? Because we truly believed that it was a good choice, because we loved it ourselves. We could describe the flavour and answer questions about it based on our own experience. We weren't being pushy or aggressive with our selling technique, and as a result it increased sales and falafel became one of our bestsellers.

Digital marketing coach Alice Benham explained this to me in the context of selling her own services:

> I don't see my marketing as pushing something because I know that what I offer is of value. I'm giving people a solution that works, for a problem that I know they struggle with. I'm giving them an opportunity to engage with something that is of genuine value to them. The more we can strip away the weird associations we have with promoting ourselves, the better. Instead, try to see it as a conversation with people who can get value from your solution.

Imagine you bump into someone who really needs to use a pen and you have one in your pocket. The logical step would be to offer them your pen, right? In fact, it would be weird if you didn't. This is how good marketing should feel.

TIP: Make a list of the typical problems your audience encounters on a regular basis. How does your product or service help them?

COMMUNICATION

When you actually sit down and think about all the ways you can sell yourself it can feel pretty... overwhelming. But the good news is that you do NOT need to cover all bases. You just need to find a few ways that work for *you*. Contrary to popular belief, not everyone should have a podcast. You don't *need* an email list with 10k subscribers. You don't *need* to write a blog post twice a week. You don't *need* to upload videos onto a YouTube channel. What you *do* need is to find a way to communicate with your audience and target market in a way that feels right to you and gets results.

Take a look at this list of the different types of communication and see which fits with your capabilities the most.

WRITTEN
If you hate the idea of seeing your own face staring back at you in a video, then that's understandable. Not because I think you're hideous or anything, but because it's only

natural. Some people – me included – communicate thoughts more clearly through the written word. In which case you have, among others, the following outlets to choose from:

- **Twitter** – for those who can write short, sharp one-liners.
- **Blogging** – generally designed for longform written content. Perfect if you want to provide helpful articles or demonstrate your knowledge on a certain topic. For example, a therapist might write articles about Cognitive Behavioural Therapy to gain trust in potential clients.
- **Emails** – a way to talk directly to people who are already interested in what you have to say. They handed over their details to you, so treat them kindly and don't spam them.
- **eBooks** – a way to package up your wisdom and give it away. You can distribute it for free as part of a marketing strategy or put a price tag on it. Yep, people still buy eBooks.... if there is something in them worth knowing that is!

AUDIO/VISUAL

Have you always sucked at writing your CV but nailed every face-to-face interview of your career? You're probably one of those annoying people who find public speaking easy too. If this sounds like you, you might like to try:

- **Podcasts** – particularly great because they're the only form of content that people can fully consume while doing something else, like walking to work or doing the housework.
- **YouTube** – a free platform where you can host videos and share them with your audience, but be warned: it's really

competitive, so you might struggle to rack up millions of views.

- **Speaking at events** – this allows you to tap into new audiences that are already established. If you're lucky, you might even get paid to speak while you promote your own services.

BIT OF BOTH

Some people are good at everything. If you're a confident writer and happy adding visuals then the world is your oyster. As well as all the options mentioned above, you can always try these out for size:

- **Online courses** – teach your audience something valuable and you might just be able to turn them into paying customers.
- **Instagram** – this has always been a visually focused platform, but well-written captions convert followers into customers.
- **Facebook** – there are still lots of businesses using it, especially those with budgets to place targeted adverts.

FINDING THE EQUILIBRIUM POINT

The most important thing is to find a combination that works for you, or, as digital marketing coach Alice Benham puts it, 'You need to find the equilibrium point – which is never going to feel perfect – between where your people are showing up and where your message is best suited.'

So, for example, if you're a photographer, then your message is probably best suited to a visual platform like Instagram. Having your own website is probably a good idea too as you can upload galleries full of images for people to browse through. But where are your audience showing up online? Perhaps they're in a local Facebook group asking for photographer recommendations, or maybe they're in a Reddit thread trying to figure out how to take a good headshot.

GET TO KNOW YOUR AUDIENCE

There's no textbook answer for what kind of marketing will work for you because every business is different. Start by thinking about your dream customer and the journey they go on before they make the decision to buy from you. Really get to know your audience and talk to them as they move through this 'customer journey'. Alice Benham explains:

The more that you can understand what that journey looks like for your people and how you can fill the gaps with content and conversation that facilitates that, that's when marketing is at its best and you're using social media for what it's made for.

Making content – whether it's written, audio-visual or both – is your way to talk to your potential and existing customers. And if you feel icky about all that sales stuff we were talking about earlier, then there's some good news here. Content marketing doesn't need to be overly salesy. In fact, I would argue that the best content marketing doesn't focus on selling at all. Instead it offers valuable information that helps build trust in your brand, which leads to more sales in the long run.

TIP: Find a way to talk to your audience regularly. Be consistent. It could be a private Facebook group, a live webinar, a monthly meet-up or an email survey. Make an effort to get to know their likes, dislikes, what motivates them and what struggles they are facing.

WHAT IS CONTENT MARKETING?

Content marketing is different from traditional marketing because it aims to provide value instead of outright selling. Traditional marketing includes adverts in magazines, on radio or TV, whereas typical content marketing includes blogs, videos, podcasts, eBooks, newsletters, infographics and webinars.

Take Emma Gannon for example. She started her podcast Ctrl Alt Delete in 2016 and has since gone on to record over 200 episodes, all of which are technically pieces of content marketing for her own personal brand. They are free to listen to (although most of them do include ad breaks) but very few of them mention her own books or services. She has used podcasting to build an engaged audience of people who are interested in listening to conversations about modern careers, so when her second book, *The Multi-Hyphen Method*, was released in 2018, it became an instant *Sunday Times* bestseller. She successfully used podcasting as a content marketing tool to increase brand awareness and connect with a large audience who were invested in her story and ready to buy her product as soon as it went on sale, without ever being an aggressive salesperson on her platform. This is the power of good content marketing.

Content marketing should do at least one of these things:

- Solve a specific problem
- Entertain
- Offer insider knowledge
- Share a unique insight
- Provide the answer to a question

The common theme here is that content marketing should be focused on what your *audience* needs. What kind of problems do your customers face on a regular basis? What self-help books do they love? What questions are they typing into Google? What stumbling blocks are they up against? The answers to these questions (and others) will help you create content that lines up with the kind of help or support they are already looking for. Your content shouldn't be one big sales pitch, which is good, because we've already established that we all hate selling. If you make your content genuinely helpful and enjoyable then you will win over your audience and they'll (eventually) want to invest in your offering with very minimal sales patter from you.

STARTING A CONVERSATION

At its most basic level, good marketing is about talking to your audience, so think about it in terms of starting a conversation. Imagine you have your dream customer sitting in front of you right now. What would the conversation be? This is a great way to brainstorm ideas for content that speaks to people in an authentic way.

For example, if you're a makeup artist, you might have a conversation about what types of foundation are best for specific skin types. You might talk about how to apply the perfect red lipstick or the importance of cleaning your makeup brushes. Covering these topics in your marketing doesn't directly address your services as a makeup artist, but it starts the conversation and shows your audience that you understand their wants and needs.

According to Alice Benham, it's this that will take your audience from 'stranger to client' in a way that doesn't feel like selling:

> *You need to begin by seeing it on that human level and understanding that even when you're promoting yourself it's better done as a story. You can imply what your solution is within a story without being overly salesy or in your face. My goal is that as soon as someone makes an enquiry with me, they are 98% ready to work with me. I couldn't tell you the last time I had an enquiry call that didn't end up with someone making a booking, because my marketing strategy is all about getting people to that place where they're ready before they book. They already know why they want to work with me and they just want to take that next step.*

BUILDING A PLATFORM

Creating good content can help you build a platform. Why do you need a platform? Well, a platform raises you up (in the same way that pint-sized Geri Halliwell gained a little height from her Buffalo trainers back in the 90s) to give you more visibility. Because you're more visible, you can reach a wider audience.

A platform isn't one thing; it's a combination of how many people read your weekly newsletter, follow you on Instagram, buy your products or watch you speak at events. It's the listeners who hear you talk on a podcast or the people who read the column you write for the weekly paper.

Your platform will consist of a variety of elements suited to your personality, your industry and, of course, what your audience prefers. Building a platform isn't easy and it takes time, but once you have it in place it's solid and you own it.

A WORD ON SOCIAL MEDIA

Having a large following on social media is great. In fact, an ODM Group study found that 74% of consumers rely on social networks to help with their purchasing decisions.[54] It's one of the most cost-effective ways to promote your business online. However, social media apps are ultimately an external service that you are using to connect with your audience, and that service can be taken away at a moment's notice. It's easy to get caught up in working hard on the app that everyone is currently using, or feeding the 'hungry ghost' that Paul Jarvis refers to in his book *Company of One*. This quest for more followers and more likes, the pursuit of exponential growth, is an insatiable appetite that can never be satisfied.

That aside, consider what happens if you wake up one morning and find out that your account has been hacked or deleted, or that the entire app has gone bust and been taken down? This is exactly what happened with Vine a few years ago, and people with millions of followers were forced to start from scratch on alternative platforms. You should try to mitigate this risk by having a platform made up of different tools, some of which are solely owned by you. Examples of this are a website, list of email subscribers, podcast or hosting your own events. This doesn't mean that you shouldn't work on building a strong social media presence; instead, you should use it as a way to point customers towards an additional way of consuming your content.

PERSONAL BRANDING

No, I'm not talking about that questionable group tattoo you and the girls got after too many sangrias when you were in Majorca '09. It's more about how you present yourself to the world.

As author Seth Godin neatly puts it: 'A brand is the set of expectations, memories, stories and relationships that, taken together, account for a consumer's decision to choose one product or service over another.'

When people visit your website, what do they read? What pictures do they see? When they follow you on Twitter, what are you talking about? When they meet you in person, what are you wearing? How do you smell? (Yes, people might infer something about you from the way you smell. Have you never caught a whiff of Tommy Girl on a grown woman? That's some confusing sh*t right there.) Even the sound of your voice can be your brand. You only have to look at someone like Oprah to see how one person can be transformed into a profitable brand.

As a freelancer, you want people to know you as the go-to person for a particular thing. You don't need to be an expert (or Oprah); you just need to have a *thing*. It could be as simple as offering tips on saving money, creating really bright makeup looks or having a passionate view on a particular subject. This doesn't mean you can't offer a variety of services; it just means that when your name pops up in conversation others instantly remember who you are based on the thing you're well known for.

SOME REAL-LIFE EXAMPLES OF PEOPLE WHO ARE NAILING PERSONAL BRANDING

SHERI SCOTT

If there's someone whose brand is synonymous with colour, it's this kween. One of the original multi-hyphenates, Sheri's Instagram account and blog appear under the name Forever Yours Betty. She is a fashion and beauty influencer but also offers services in events, digital PR and social media strategy. With so many areas of expertise, her personal brand ties everything together seamlessly with one thing: the colour orange. Check out her Instagram account @foreveryoursbetty to see what I mean.

ANNA WHITEHOUSE

Anna started a parenting blog called Mutha Pukka, which has been hugely successful. She is passionate about making flexible working commonplace (a girl after my own heart) and campaigns for this under the name Flex Appeal.

She's done flash mobs, written a book, has a slot on Heart Radio and works tirelessly to get the government to take flexible working seriously. Yes, she's got a swish website and a quirky dress sense, but her brand is built around a core element: her passion for change. This is what makes her likeable and memorable.

LAURA JANE WILLIAMS

Author of *Becoming*, *Ice Cream for Breakfast* and *Our Stop*, Laura has become known for her craft. From her dating advice in *Grazia*, her monthly column in *Red* to her beautifully penned Instagram captions, she consistently demonstrates her ability to write creatively on a professional level. She uses social media as an artform, a way to express emotion and connect with people on a deeper level. In a piece for *Red* magazine, she writes:

'That's what the platform [Instagram] is about – taking the smallest and most ordinary moments of your day and capturing them with your iPhone, making artists out of us all. Using Instagram properly means training your eye to see the story everywhere you go. Instagram can, in fact, make us more in tune with our world, not less.'[55]

This ability to inject a poetic quality into her online presence is undoubtedly an element of why many people have become fans of Laura's online courses and published work.

QUESTIONS TO ASK ABOUT YOUR OWN PERSONAL BRANDING

How do you want people to feel when they interact with your brand?

- What do you want to be known for?
- What are you most skilled at?
- What's a quirky aspect of your life worth sharing?
- Is there a colour/symbol/theme that defines your brand?
- How are you different from your competitors?
- What are your customers struggling with?
- What solution can you provide them?

Use these answers to inform the content that you create, from the tone of your Instagram captions to the images in your blog posts. It can even help you make bigger decisions such as which brands to affiliate yourself with and how you price your services.

DOS AND DON'TS OF SELLING YOURSELF

DO TALK TO PEOPLE IRL

As the saying goes, 'People do business with people they know, like, and trust', so if your clients are local to you then it's worth organising regular meetings to stay in touch. While building this rapport will help solidify your client list, it will also give you that much-needed real-people connection that is missing from your lonely home office.

Talk to everyone about what you do. Journalist Michelle Gately found herself explaining her content-writing abilities to her new osteopath and, after a few sessions, he signed up to become one of her clients. 'As a freelance writer or journalist, almost any conversation you have could lead to a story either directly or by sparking something for further investigation,' says Michelle. 'It's the same principle with any business. You never know how talking about your business, or even just your skills in general, could lead to a new client or a new opportunity.'

DO CREATE A BUZZ AROUND A NEW LAUNCH

When there is a special discount on something you're interested in but the discount is time-limited, this can trigger something psychologists call 'anticipatory regret'. Yep, you anticipate that you will regret not capitalising on the discounted offer and this pushes you into making a purchase. It sounds a bit manipulative, but there are ethical ways to use this tool to encourage customers who are already interested to take action.

I spoke to Vix Meldrew, who experimented with opening and closing the doors to her membership site Grow & Glow, and although there was no monetary discount, she saw results from simply implementing a time frame:

> *I opened up my membership site with an initial limit of 100 members and they all sold within fifty-eight minutes. I did not expect that. Then I closed the membership. Later on I opened the doors again and we ended up with 350 members and left the doors open and the memberships were just trickling in. So I weighed it up and thought, actually, I quite like the launch model and that works for us.*

Here are some examples that might work for you:

- Set a specific date for a group workshop instead of waiting on an individual or business to hire you
- Offer a select few early-bird tickets to an event
- Sell a limited number of one-off products
- Limit the number of clients you take on and let your audience know every time a slot gets filled
- Offer a discount that runs out after a certain amount of time

DO SHARE THE RESULTS OF WHAT YOU DO

This is what Vix Meldrew does to prove to her audience that her current members are getting value from her services. 'I feel like with Grow & Glow, when you're selling expertise and a community, actually just showing off what the community is like does the selling for me,' she says. 'Sharing those positive testimonials and results is what encourages people to sign up.'

When I'm working on a project I'm really proud of, I always share it on social media, whether it's an article I've had published in a magazine or an Instagram account I've been managing for a client. I find that showing the fruits of my labour is much more effective than simply talking about the services I offer, because it proves to people that a) I know what I'm doing and b) people are already willing to hire me.

Other examples of this include:

- Creating a page on your website to showcase your best work
- Sharing statistics that prove your work gets tangible results

If you just copy what someone else is doing it will never fully connect with you or your audience because it's not authentic.

- Shouting about your successes, whether that's an industry award or a mention in a magazine
- Sharing customer testimonials
- Giving your current clients a shout-out on social media and encouraging people to go look at the work you do for them

DON'T COPY AND PASTE FROM YOUR COMPETITORS

It's tempting to see what other people are doing and replicate their marketing strategy for your own business. While it's great to see what's out there, you've got to find a way of selling that aligns with your personal beliefs. If you just copy what someone else is doing it will never fully connect with you or your audience because it's not authentic.

If you've found a strategy or technique that seems to work for your competitors, ask yourself:

- Is this the best way to communicate my message to my specific audience?
- How can I adapt it to make it unique to my business?
- Does it align with my personality and how I do business?
- Can I take the idea and execute it on a different platform?

Researching your competitors is a good exercise, but tread with caution. People aren't stupid and they will notice if you are ripping off someone else's ideas and they'll judge you for it. If something feels too close to call, go back to the drawing board.

DON'T FORGET YOUR ROOTS

Having a personal story behind your business is what sets you apart from everyone else. According to Alice Benham, when you opt out of letting your audience into your world, you're 'doing yourself a disservice by not realising the role that your story plays in people wanting your solution'.

Chances are, what you're selling isn't totally unique and your audience could go elsewhere to find it. By incorporating your own experience and values, you add a much-needed dose of humanity to your services.

DON'T EXPECT PEOPLE TO BUY BEFORE THEY'RE READY

A savvy freelancer plays the long game. Instead of pressuring people into purchasing, accompany them through their journey by offering knowledge and support until they are ready to invest. Alice Benham summed this up beautifully when I asked her about it:

> *You really want to build something that aligns with your values and you want to wake up every morning and feel really good about how you show up online and what you're sharing. You'll feel confident that everyone who is choosing to work with you is doing it for the right reasons.*

CHECKLIST

- Really believe in what you're selling (if you can't, start selling something that you believe in!)
- Think about how you communicate best with your audience
- Create content with purpose
- Think about how you can send a message with your personal branding

CHAPTER 17

INCREASING REVENUE

We've already talked about making ends meet, but that hand-to-mouth state of being is something that I'm personally keen to see in my rear-view mirror.

Don't get me wrong. I do not want to be rich. I do not want to build an empire. I do not want to have premises and staff members and merchandise (although if that's your dream, hats off to you, babe). I just want to increase my income steadily over time, in the same way that my salary would increase if I was working in traditional employment.

I want to see the fruits of my labour, but without a boss to give me a raise, I'm going to have to sort that out for myself. I want to be able to buy the moisturiser that I like instead of the cheaper dupe. I want to shop in Zara for dresses and buy Calvin Klein underwear, the kind that's so fancy it's sold on an individual hanger and not stuffed into a vacuum-sealed multipack.

God damnit, I want to buy the BIG White Company candle and burn it all day long, guilt-free.

You might think that it's a good idea to charge 20% less than your competitors, but you'll still be expected to deliver the same standard of work.

FINANCIAL WELLBEING

Making more money is something that many of us feel guilty about. We got into freelancing for the love of the job, man, not for the dollar! Okay, but there's only so long that you can survive on your passion and at some point you'll realise that increasing your income is going to have a direct result on your wellbeing.

The problem with not making enough money is that it forces you to work harder and longer to make up the deficit. You might think that it's a good idea to charge 20% less than your competitors, but you'll still be expected to deliver the same standard of work. You'll also have to find that extra money somewhere, so you'll seek out more clients, but then you'll have less time, so you'll end up working evenings and weekends to get everything done. Then you'll be offered a great PR opportunity overseas but you won't have enough money or time to go on the trip, so you'll turn it down and you'll feel frustrated. You may even develop a grudge against your clients, which affects your relationship with them and the quality of work you deliver. Because you're charging so little and working so much, you'll have no time to promote yourself, find higher-paying clients or learn new skills. This will likely lead to a lack in job satisfaction and burnout. Before you know it you're at the end of your tether and need time off and therapy but, guess what? You can't afford either.

Do you obsessively check your bank balance multiple times a day? Or, worse, do you avoid checking it altogether because you don't want to know how bad the situation is? These are signs that your finances are a stressor in your life.

You're not alone. A study by Leapers found that for independent workers, irregular income and the general cost of living were the top most significant stressors around work.[56] I believe that improving your financial wellbeing is related to practicality and mindset, and that there are lots of ways you can take action to ease anxiety about money, many of which can be found in Chapter 13.

As well as managing the admin side of your finances (e.g. tracking your expenses, sending invoices, getting paid on time), taking steps to increase your income over time is – I think – a key aspect of feeling financially stable. It's generally accepted that a freelancer's income will fluctuate from month to month, but I think it's only right that you should expect to see an increase in overall profits year on year. Growing your business doesn't have to mean expanding by outsourcing, franchising or adding more and endless strings to your bow. I believe you can increase your income slowly by implementing a few – or maybe all – of these tips.

UPSELLING

You know when you're in Starbucks and all you want is an oat milk flat white, but the cute barista asks if you would like anything else today and somehow you hear yourself ordering an almond croissant even though you said today was going to be the day you gave up sugar? That's upselling.

Obviously, you don't want to sell your customers things that they don't want (although I think we can all accept that I truly did want the almond croissant), so upsell with caution. Having a good handle on your services is key, so that when you're talking to customers you can easily offer add-ons in a way that feels natural and genuinely helpful.

EXAMPLES OF UPSELLING:

You're writing a one-off press release for a client and notice that there are a lot of typos on their website.
Upsell: Proofreading service.

You meet for coffee to interview the CEO of a start-up for a feature you're writing and uncover that she has no social media presence.
Upsell: Write some LinkedIn posts for her profile.

You're doing a nutrition plan for a client and she expresses an interest in vegan baking.
Upsell: A copy of your vegan recipe book.

You're approached by a hotel to stay a night and post a review on social media.
Upsell: A five-minute video that they can use as part of their marketing campaigns.

UPDATE YOUR OFFERING

When you're just starting out as a freelancer it might take a while to figure out what it is you actually do. In the early days I did anything that people asked me to do (within reason, obviously), which meant I ended up doing things that I wasn't good at or things that fried my brain. I wrote a lot of copy for voucher code websites one summer and it made me very sad indeed. One year later I was writing about social media tips for plumbers and having a whale of a time.

My point is, don't be afraid to change up what you do, because when you find what you're passionate about (or really good at), you'll earn more money. People will pay more because your work is better and they'll come back repeatedly or recommend you to others because your service is so good.

PRACTICAL WAYS THAT YOU CAN UPDATE YOUR OFFERING:

- Think about your audience. Do you have hundreds of thousands of followers? If so, can you sell something low-cost that they would all buy, like T-shirts, an eBook or a webinar? If you have a small audience, then how can your offering support one or two individuals? Can you offer a one-to-one personalised package that requires a larger investment on their part?
- Send a survey to your existing clients to find out what they need help with. Can you solve their problem with a service or product?
- Create a bundle of all your most popular items and knock a percentage off the price.
- Offer a service targeted at a specific customer based on your expert knowledge. For example, are you a hairdresser with children who love wild and wacky styles? You could offer tutorials for parents or group styling parties for kids.
- Invest in training to back up your credentials so you can charge more.
- Learn a new skill so that you can offer additional services.
- Take your online audience offline by arranging a live event.

CUSTOMER SERVICE

According to accounting software company Sage, when a company offers good customer service, 86% of people will pay more and 89% of those who experienced bad service will go directly to a competitor.[57] Loyal customers are worth ten times what they initially spend with you (*ten times!*), so it's well worth nurturing existing customers, as it should pay off in the long term. If you're not thinking about how you serve your customers, then you might be earning less money.

I spoke to journalist Hattie Crisell, who has been working in freelance roles on and off for over ten years. She says that delivering a good service is one of the best things you can do in order to maximise your chances of getting more work. 'You've got to be a safe pair of hands,' she told me. 'When you're self-employed you want people to keep coming back to you again and again, so you've got to be easy to work with, reliable and do exactly what you've been asked to do.'

Lots of people can probably do the job that you do, so you've got to add that extra cherry on top by making life easier for the people you work with. When Hattie was acting features director at *Grazia*, she was in the position to pick and choose the freelancers she commissioned and she often favoured those who had done a good job previously: 'All that stuff helps because when I was an editor the people who caused me the least stress were the people I wanted to work with again and again.'

HOW TO GIVE BETTER CUSTOMER SERVICE:

- Send out a handwritten note to every new customer. You could even go one step further and send them a personalised gift like cookies or a mug with their name on it. (I don't know why, but people love stuff with their name on it.)

- If you sell a product, consider hand packaging to make sure that items arrive in pristine condition. Add in a discount code for future purchases.
- Be responsive. Fifty per cent of consumers give brands one week to respond to questions before they take their business elsewhere. If you struggle to keep up with multiple social platforms, use auto-responders to tell people where to send customer queries.
- Set out in writing exactly what you'll deliver to your client or customer so that they aren't disappointed with what they receive. Then try to go the extra mile to make them feel extra special. For example, I try to send journalism pieces twenty-four hours before the final deadline because I know editors appreciate writers who file promptly. If you're sending out a package, advise that it might take up to seven days and then send it out ASAP. Any way that you can pleasantly surprise people is a bonus.
- Communicate regularly. Clients love to know that you are regularly working on their stuff, so keep them updated by email, even if it's just a quick rundown of tasks you've completed recently. Don't forget the power of a face-to-face meet-up or video chat when it comes to building strong relationships with others.
- Say thank you. Once you've done business with someone, remember to show gratitude that they chose to hire you. Do this personally and shout about them on social media for extra brownie points.
- Offer incentives or rewards. Make people feel part of your inner circle by offering them early access, free content, discounts or freebies.

> TIP: The more you know about your individual customers, the better you can serve them. Take time to genuinely build up business relationships by sending personalised messages, emails, sharing their work and meeting up in real life.

INCREASE YOUR RATES

Okay, so there is one sure-fire way that I've yet to mention that will make you more money almost instantly: put your prices up. In my experience this is the thing that every freelancer needs to get better at, including myself. It's easy to find clients if you start out by undercutting the competition, but working for pennies is unsustainable, so at some point you'll need to raise your rates.

Even if you started out charging what was the industry standard a few years back, an increase will be due to keep up with inflation – not to mention the fact that you should have gained more experience and credibility as a freelancer. (If you're *not* better at your job after a few years, then that's a whole other problem and may be worth addressing before you put your prices up.)

So, here are my tips on increasing your rates with existing clients:

GIVE PLENTY OF WARNING
Sending an email simply dictating your new rates probably won't go down well, so put out the feelers in a polite way. Let them know that you plan to put your rates up in a specific

time frame, like the next ninety days, or when the new financial year starts.

SET UP A CONVERSATION

Putting your rates up is more likely to go down well if you invite clients to engage in a conversation. It gives you a chance to explain your process and reasoning for the increase and have a back and forth, allowing them to ask questions if they want.

Talking to someone face to face about money might seem the scariest way to approach this, but in reality it just humanises the entire thing. You'll be surprised at how quickly the initial tension will dissolve once you're both sat having a grown-up discussion about money. To make it nicer, add coffee and cake.

Having a negotiation is fine, but if the client starts to get passive-aggressive, try to be polite. After the interaction you might want to consider how you can drop this client long-term, because they clearly don't value your work.

DO YOUR RESEARCH AND CITE EXAMPLES IF POSSIBLE

Do not just pluck a figure out of thin air and expect your client to blindly accept the increase. Chances are they still want to work with you (it's easier than finding a replacement, right?), but they're not going to pay too much above the industry standard to keep you, unless you're head and shoulders above the rest or delivering unbeatable results. Don't take them for a chump. They can research your competitors and find out what they're charging, so you should do the same. This will give you a range of figures to work within, taking into account what your current rate is.

For example, if your current day rate is £300 and the industry average is closer to £600, you've got some wriggle room.

However, be honest; do you realistically think that the client is going to double their spend to pay for you? Major corporations might have the capacity, but smaller businesses are likely paying £300 because that's what they can afford. My advice? Split the difference and ask for £450, laying out the figures previously mentioned so that the client can see how you arrived at that figure as a result of actual research. Transparency will go a long way to convincing them that you're not taking the p*ss.

BUILD YOUR OWN FREELANCER'S SELECTION BOX

I think that one of the best insurance policies you can build for yourself is an income made up of multiple options.

Everyone loves a Mars bar. Ideally we'd have endless Mars bars, but sometimes they are thin on the ground, especially if someone has nicked one from your selection box while you weren't looking. Sometimes you need to opt for something else, like a bag of Maltesers. When push comes to shove, at some point, you're going to have to settle for the one you like the least, like a Bounty or a Bournville. I know. Life is tough.

Having all these options on offer means that you'll never go hungry. You won't get the same enjoyment from every choice, but hey, at least you'll always have options.

WAYS YOU CAN ADD DIFFERENT INCOME STREAMS TO YOUR BUSINESS:

- Public speaking
- Physical products
- Coaching/training/mentoring

- Hosting your own events
- Workshops
- Advertising on your website
- Sponsored content
- Consultancy
- eBooks
- Online courses
- Live webinars
- Membership site
- Agency work

You don't have to be an expert, and there are plenty of online courses and tutorials that will help inform you about how to get started in new areas of business. Also, you don't need to dedicate a huge portion of your time to one income stream for it to be profitable. For example, I probably do about ten public speaking gigs a year, but each one can earn me several hundred pounds. I don't actively seek them out, but I've spent time honing my skills so that when I do get an offer, I'm ready to snap it up and bump up my income that month.

CHECKLIST

- Learn to upsell to your existing clients
- Increase your rates with existing clients
- Regularly evaluate and update your offering
- Give top-notch customer service
- Build your own Freelancer's Selection Box of income streams

CHAPTER 18

BEING YOUR BEST (PRODUCTIVE) SELF

I have a real problem with the concept of productivity. On one hand, I pride myself on being able to bang out a few thousand words each day in spite of my sheer inability to type quickly and my lack of formal qualifications in the English language. On the other, I am deeply concerned by our society's need to make people produce things in order to feel worthy. The student who reads the most books is praised. The most effective salesperson always gets the bonus. The mum who is always cleaning and baking is the "perfect" role model.

I really had to wrangle with my productivity obsession when I was off work with depression because the guilt of being home, doing *nothing*, was hard to bear. I went from juggling staff rotas, ordering stock, hosting training days and managing a department with a turnover of over half a million pounds to watching the sun rise and fall from my bed. The sixteen-hour sleepathons were essential self-care though, and proof that no one can sustain a ludicrously high level of productivity forever. After years of being powered by Irn Bru, flapjacks and the need to impress anyone in my wake, I went from 100% to zero. Complete exhaustion.

Being productive isn't about being busy all the time; it's about getting the most out of the time you have.

I'm not exhausted anymore, but I've learnt my lesson. I won't sacrifice my health in order to maximise my output, but that's just made me more interested in the whole concept of productivity. Being productive isn't about being busy all the time; it's about getting the most out of the time you have. In the words of Emma Gannon, I want to find ways to 'work less and create more' as a freelancer.

I didn't leave one stressful career to create another one in my own home. No, siree. (For that reason, the chapter following this one is about why your mental health needs to be a top priority.)

This chapter on productivity should not be taken verbatim. If you're too mentally unwell to get stuff done, that's okay. The amount of work you manage to do on the days when you're feeling 100% doesn't set the bar for every single day of the rest of your life. There will be days when you do nothing, and that's not necessarily a bad thing. It's good actually, because you need time off, which we'll talk about later. You'll always have productivity peaks and troughs because – guess what? – you're only human.

FINDING A ROUTINE THAT WORKS FOR YOU

According to research,[58] 40% of self-employed people see themselves as more productive outside the traditional 9-to-5. If it were up to me I would work from lunchtime until about 8 pm, but my husband comes home around six and we have dinner together so it makes sense for me to stop work then too. However I do think that one of the great things about the OOO lifestyle is that you can work whenever you want. Routine is not enforced and, call me crazy, I like that.

If I have a bout of insomnia (which happens every few weeks), I get up and do some work. I quite often do boring admin tasks until 5 am and then sleep the rest of the day because I've done all my work in the middle of the night. It's not a healthy cycle long-term, but once in a while I think it's just fine. It keeps life exciting. If you think waking up at 3 pm is exciting (which I do). You feel a bit like you're beating the system because you earn a day off by working through the night – kind of like the freelancer equivalent of Time Off In Lieu or the much-anticipated Snow Day at school.

Research from Barclays Bank says that the most productive time for small- to medium-sized enterprises is 2:23 am,[59] and I'm like, *fully* on board with that data. When I'm working on a creative project, ideas present themselves to me with striking – if slightly inconvenient – clarity between midnight and 3 am.

I guess I do have a routine of sorts, it's just not the stereotypical yoga-before-sunrise-followed-by-a-honey-bran-muffin kinda routine. But it works for me. I know there are some freelancers who wake up at the same time every morning, have the same breakfast, go for coffee and lunch breaks at set times and clock off at 5 pm on the dot. Some have set days for certain clients and schedule co-working days at the same time each week. I get why this is appealing, and I have tried it. I even made a spreadsheet where I assigned certain tasks to every day, but as soon as other jobs came up (as they always do in freelancing, when you least expect them), it threw out my carefully arranged timetable. Then I felt like a failure. I didn't spend Monday morning researching keywords like I had planned, then I didn't write the blog post in the afternoon. I would spend another hour trying to rearrange the whole thing only for something else to crop up and ruin my plans again. No, that kind of routine does not take my fancy at all. My kind of routine is just making small promises to myself that I have to fulfil at some point in the day. For example:

- I promise I will shower today.
- I promise I will eat a vegetable today.
- I promise I will leave the house today.
- I promise I will write 500 words today.

I'm not an advert for routines, but I will admit that science proves me wrong on their effectiveness. Routines encourage good habits, provide structure, increase efficiency and improve motivation. But that doesn't mean you need to do the same thing day in, day out; you just need to find your flow. And what routine works for you in March might not work in April or May. Don't be afraid to switch things up for a few weeks to see if a different routine gives you a new lust for life!

I think author Elizabeth Gilbert put it eloquently in a blog post she wrote about the creative process in the context of writing, although I believe it's a sentiment that is applicable to anyone who needs to be a self-motivator:

As for discipline – it's important, but sort of over-rated. The more important virtue for a writer, I believe, is self-forgiveness. Because your writing will always disappoint you. Your laziness will always disappoint you. You will make vows: 'I'm going to write for an hour every day,' and then you won't do it. You will think: 'I suck,

I'm such a failure. I'm washed-up.' Continuing to write after that heartache of disappointment doesn't take only discipline, but also self-forgiveness.[60]

FINDING YOUR TIME TO SHINE

In the first few months of freelancing, as the novelty began to wear off and my morning enthusiasm decreased rapidly, I had a lot of unproductive days. Days where I would do *anything* but work. Instead of pitching feature ideas to magazines, I would make huge batches of soup. Instead of looking for new clients, I would clean the skirting boards. Instead of doing my tax return, I would arrange my books alphabetically and then rearrange them again by colour.

Having an unproductive day can be annoying in the short term, but in the long term it can be a necessary evil in accepting that your concentration levels are unpredictable. It also makes you hyper-aware of the hours when you knock it out of the park productivity-wise. Those days when you barely look up from your screen, when you forget to eat or even go to the bathroom for hours on end. Those days when you genuinely forget for a few hours that you even have a phone. I promise, those days do exist, and they can give you a real insight into what conditions lend themselves to you feeling focused and in the zone. It's just a case of noticing when these moments occur and trying to unpick the reasons or set of circumstances that led up to your glorious productivity triumphs.

Personally, I'm most productive:

- On long train rides (going from Birmingham to Glasgow is four solid hours of writing bliss!)
- After one cup of Starbucks Cold Brew
- After a few sips of an Espresso Martini
- At the weekends because no one is sending me emails
- In a coffee shop between 8 am and 12 noon
- At home between 4 pm and 6 pm
- Twenty-four hours before a deadline, regardless of location or the beverage in my hand

Finding the things that spark you into focus-mode takes time and practice, but once you start figuring them out you'll be hooked and intent on finding more of them. When I started writing this book I plotted out various places I could visit by train to drink in that sweet travel time that seems to work magic on my writing. I've written on trains to Fort William, Liverpool, Cardiff and Manchester. I've written on my phone on the Tube and in the back seat of my parents' car on the way to St Andrews. What can I say? I have a thing for moving vehicles.

> TIP: Every week, make an effort to try a new workspace. It could be a different room in the house, a new coffee shop or an entirely different city. Observe whether you work better or worse in that location.

KEEPING A PRODUCTIVITY JOURNAL

Writing a diary has long been known as an effective self-reflective tool. I used to keep one as a teenager and I have always written my experiences down in some shape or form, and I generally have one or two different journals on the go at any one time. While I don't particularly want to reflect on that awkward first kiss I detailed over three and a half pages when I was twelve years old, I have found it helpful to keep a log of my productivity levels.

Keeping a productivity journal offers a set of qualitative data that you can use to observe your own habits and behaviours in a way that you can't really do otherwise. It's hard to notice the small things happening every day. If you're struggling to figure out the ingredients that make your productivity levels rise, make a note of anything you did that day that might have played a part. Even if it seems insignificant (like an extra shot of espresso in your coffee or jam on your toast instead of butter), record it anyway. The power comes when you observe this data over time. You'll start to see patterns forming that will point you in the right direction. When I did this I realised that, amazingly, I feel more awake when I drink green tea first thing in the morning instead of coffee. I found that getting up earlier than 8 am was counterproductive. I realised that taking a break in the afternoon was essential if I wanted to feel less anxious in the evening and that yoga – well, it actually really works.

TIP: Keep a productivity diary every day for two weeks detailing your actions and behaviours every hour or so.

> Include information on what you drink, eat, what location you work from and what kind of exercise you do. Write a sentence or two about how you feel each day in relation to the work you're producing. Now you have all the information you need to start tweaking your own schedule to make the most of every day.

AVOIDING DISTRACTIONS

Sometimes being productive isn't about learning to increase your output, it's really about avoiding distractions. When I filled out my productivity journal I found that (shocker) I was wasting a lot of my working day scrolling through social media. (I've found a few ways to help with this, which I've detailed below.) I was also getting distracted by tasks at home such as tidying up and doing the washing up. When I feel these behaviours creeping in, I now notice them and normally leave the house to work in a coffee shop instead.

So, here are a few tips on how to be more productive by avoiding distractions:

- Don't look at your inbox until you've done something productive first. This guarantees you'll have done at least one thing that matters before getting distracted.
- Delete the email app off your phone. You never know what you're going to find when you click on that evil little icon, so don't do it until you have the time to fully engage with requests and enquiries.

- Forget inbox zero. Instead, deal with the most important emails first and file the rest in folders, prioritising the ones that need to be actioned first. (See Chapter 13 for more on this.)
- Limit your access to the internet by unplugging your WiFi while you work (as long as you don't actually *need* it of course). There is also an app called Freedom which allows you to stay online but block the use of specific websites.
- Delete all the apps on your phone that are designed for endless scrolling. Twitter, Facebook, Pinterest, Instagram and Reddit are just a few that spring to mind. You can always reinstall them later.
- Use the Forest App to set a timer on your phone. This stops you from scrolling and reminds you to get on with work until the timer is finished. Alternatively, put your phone in flight mode and set a timer to encourage you to stop scrolling.
- Do a brain dump to get all your mental distractions out of your head and on to paper. List everything that's on your mind – whether it's work or personal – and go back to it later after you've dealt with the task at hand.

HOW TO PRIORITISE

Being a freelancer means that there is often a long, long list of things that need to be done. From client work to trying out that new SEO tool or scheduling social media posts, it seems like there is always something that needs to be addressed. While it's true that this list will always be growing, you can alleviate the pressure by acknowledging that not everything on this never-ending list is urgent.

Learning to prioritise your daily to-do lists is a skill that needs to be mastered, especially if you feel like you're constantly working without an end in sight. Here are a few tips that help me organise my tasks:

ORGANISE BY DUE DATE

How often have you found yourself answering emails that feel urgent when you've actually got a piece of client work due in twenty-four hours? Prioritise your to-do list on a due-date basis, and you can rest assured that there's nothing more pressing lingering in the background that you should be doing instead.

AIM FOR SMUG LEVEL 100

There are plenty of jobs that we don't want to do but, after they're done, we'll make sure everyone knows about it. Maybe it's going to a spin class (requires Tweeting about before, during and after) or doing your tax return six months before the deadline. I hate doing my tax return (doesn't everyone?), but the sense of satisfaction afterwards is worth it. The first person I text is my friend Emily, because I know that her dad makes a point of doing his tax return on Christmas Day. So I know that doing mine in July is slightly better and I secretly hope that this information makes its way back to Emily's dad – Emily's dad, whom I have never met, yet will always truly admire.

TREAT YO'SELF

When I sit down to a meal I always go in with a strategy. (Yes, I take mealtimes very seriously – get over it.) I always want to leave the best till last. I want my last mouthful to be the tastiest part of the meal, whether it's the crispiest roast potato or the cheesiest corner of pizza. Other people (I'm looking at you, husband) choose to eat the best bit first. It just depends on how your mind works. So sometimes, I prioritise my tasks to make sure that I always go out on a high. While writing this book I've often set aside a Friday afternoon to go to the local Wetherspoons (classy) and enjoy a large glass of wine while I write. When I'm struggling to get motivated, I pick the most fun task and do that first. The beauty of being freelance is that you can arrange your day to suit you, so why not take advantage of it?

RECLAIM YOUR FINEST HOUR

Pinpointing which part of your day is the most productive will change the way you work. Once you identify your finest hour, you can arrange your tasks to make the most of when you're at your best instead of trying to work at 100% when you're feeling more like 6%. It's like trying to do yoga when you're slightly hungover. Your balance is all off, doing downward-facing dog makes you want to vomit and when you close your eyes to meditate all you can think about is that embarrassing text message you sent last night to your old boss proclaiming that she is the Michelle Obama of human resources. You're not your best self and it is not your finest hour. For example, admin tasks don't need you to be fully charged; you can easily input figures into a spreadsheet if your battery is flashing red. But a client call to talk about your strategy for the next financial year? You'd better bring your A-game. This is a task for your finest hour.

You finest hour is the part of the day during which:

- Work flows easily
- There are fewer (ideally zero) distractions
- You have the most energy
- You feel inspired
- You love yourself

Knowing when your finest hour is gives you a starting point to piece together the rest of your day. It allows you to slot in your most important work at the peak of your day and draws attention to when your energy dips. This is a good thing! Energy comes and goes, and that's okay. When you know that you always get tired at 2 pm, you'll start to acknowledge this as a part of life. You might even lean into your natural rhythm and take a nap instead of staring at your screen for two hours and feeling guilty about your lack of creativity. This is a form of self-acceptance that many freelancers refuse to practise, but something that I believe is the key to happiness when you work for yourself.

SUPERCHARGE YOUR FINEST HOUR

Once you've located your finest hour and kept a productivity journal, you can marry the two. Say, for example, you've identified that your finest hour occurs at 9 am. It's been working pretty well because there are zero distractions (you haven't opened your inbox yet), but you struggle to get creative work done because you're not a morning person. According to your productivity journal, you feel most inspired to get into creative work after you've listened to 90s pop music. My advice? Crank Britney Spears' best work while you get ready to start *your* work and see if it gets your juices flowing. I don't drink coffee in the morning, but if I need to supercharge my finest hour I will get myself to Starbucks for a cold brew. There is something in that mystical elixir (probably the caffeine; it's not really a secret, is it?) that gets me excited about whatever I'm working on.

Hilary Rowland, co-founder of Boom Cycle, says that she is more motivated after a workout, which I actually think is genius, something I'm going to try ASAP. In an article for Get The Gloss, she was quoted as saying, 'I can think more clearly and the added endorphin buzz puts a rosy glow on everything while boosting my confidence.'[61]

Here are some other ways to supercharge your finest hour:

- Listen to focus music while you work (there are loads of free ones on YouTube)
- Turn off the WiFi if you don't need it
- Schedule in a reward afterwards (e.g. an episode of your favourite podcast or very buttery toast, OR BOTH)
- Have a nap beforehand
- Set a timer with an alarm

PRODUCTIVITY HACKS

Obviously, there is more than just one hour in your working day, so finding ways to maximise the rest of your time is an essential part of being a freelancer. Being a one-man/girl band means that you will have a lot of tasks to juggle, and it can seem like there's always a new social media platform to sign up to or a new marketing trick to try out. However, you've got to feel in control of your day if you want to get sh*t done. Here are a few hacks to try:

SET A TIMER

For non-essential tasks or ones that drag you down a never-ending rabbit hole (research, reading, data entry), set a timer for thirty minutes and then stop when the time is up. Otherwise you'll spend all day faffing about.

USE THE TOMATO TECHNIQUE

Okay, it's technically called the Pomodoro Technique (named after a tomato-shaped timer). Either way, it's about using set intervals of intense concentration to get more work done. First, you set a timer for twenty-five minutes and work without distractions on the task at hand. Once the timer ends, put a tick on a piece of paper, then take a five-minute break. Go on, pick up your phone and get all that scrolling out of your system. Then reset the timer and repeat until you have four ticks on your paper. Then enjoy an extended break of up to thirty minutes and repeat the whole system. It's the breaks that give you the mental space to keep working, so make sure you actually use them.

OVER-ESTIMATE

When planning out your day, assume that most tasks will take double the amount of time you think they will. This takes the pressure off to do things quickly, meaning that you'll make fewer mistakes and maybe even get finished up early.

TAKE A NAP

It might seem counterproductive, but a NASA study found that a forty-minute nap improved performance and alertness in military pilots and astronauts (by 34% and 100% respectively). You may not be an astronaut, but you do deserve to be more alert, so try out a wee afternoon nap and see how it makes you feel.

HAVE A KARAOKE SESSION

Singing is a natural antidepressant, reduces stress levels and improves mental alertness. I've been known to pull up karaoke videos on YouTube when I'm experiencing that dreaded afternoon slump. Personal favourites? Anything by Alanis Morrisette or Avril Lavigne.

TAKE AN AFTERNOON SHOWER

God, there is nothing more glorious than realising that working from home means you can shower at the drop of a hat. Have you ever noticed that all your best ideas come to you when you're diligently massaging in your Aussie 3-Minute Miracle conditioner? That's because showers are magic. A hot shower will also increase your dopamine levels, which is helpful, as that's the 'neurotransmitter that our brain produces to nudge us into doing stuff'.[62] It's great in the morning, but why not take advantage of it when you feel yourself careering into that midday period when you can't think straight?

USE CAFFEINE STRATEGICALLY

I'm a caffeine nightmare. I love coffee. I love the taste, I love sitting in cafés (I think I was French in a former life) and I love the pep in my step. But I'm also a highly anxious person and caffeine makes that worse. But, here's the kicker: I'm not a morning person. Like, I will threaten my husband with murder if he dares to hold a conversation with me before I'm fully awake. So caffeine sucks me in. I love it, but it doesn't always love me.

After I decided to keep a diary for a week while I experimented with caffeine, however, I figured out that coffee in the morning doesn't actually help me. It makes me anxious and worried and I just want to avoid all responsibilities and go back to bed. Green tea, on the other hand, hydrates me and offers a steady but manageable caffeine hit (yes, green tea has caffeine in it), which eases me into the day with zero nerve damage.

I realised, though, that I was getting an afternoon slump. So I tried having a coffee at around 2 pm, just before my slump took hold. Apparently if you wait until you're actually tired, caffeine has no effect — it's too late. So drinking at 2 pm lifted my energy before it crashed, and that made sure I was still fully functioning until the end of the day.

It's easy to lean on caffeine and habitually drink it first thing in the morning. For a few days drink water instead, and save coffee for midmorning or just before a workout. Do you feel more focused? Has your output increased? Or are you completely useless without an early energy boost? These experiments will help you make informed decisions about whether that third espresso is truly making you feel more awake or if it's simply a pattern that could be changed for the better.

SET A THEME FOR THE DAY

As a freelancer, you have to wear a lot of hats. This week, for example, my tasks have included graphic design, writing, editing, research and hosting an online training session. I've also had admin tasks to do, like going to the post office, answering emails and making phone calls.

The energy it takes to switch from one mode to another is draining. Each task switch might waste only one tenth of a second, but if you do a lot of switching in a day it can add up to a loss of 40% of your productivity.[63] To counter this, lots of successful freelancers benefit from setting a theme each day. For example:

Monday: Admin
Tuesday: Meetings
Wednesday: Content creation
Thursday: Research
Friday: Client calls

Looking at this weekly plan might give you an idea as to why your current schedule isn't working. Have you ever come out of an intense meeting and tried to sit down to do something creative? I personally find that experience as effective/successful as trying to find a party dress in TK MAXX. It takes hours, it's stressful as hell and the results are always disappointing. I'll be honest, theme setting is much easier if you are good at saying no. I'm the worst for getting an urgent email from a client at 10 am asking for work to be delivered on the same day, and when that happens whatever theme I had planned goes out the window. However, you can negate this scenario by refusing to look at your inbox until you've done the most important task that day.

TRY COLOUR-CODING

If you're not into day themes, try planning your days in colour. I find this helpful because I work with multiple clients, so when I assign a task to a day I highlight it in a particular colour. Then when I look at my week I can see how much time I'm spending on each project.

I also highlight my self-care moments in pink by way of reminding myself that these are fun parts of the week that shouldn't be cancelled. It can be easy to work late every night as a freelancer, but when I glance down and see the word 'movie night' highlighted in pink, I always seem to get my work finished on time!

I highlight deadlines in bright orange as this helps me prioritise my work and reminds me to turn down (or at least space out) extra work if it comes in too close to another one.

MAKE LISTS

You know that satisfying feeling you get when you score something off your to-do list? Make that a regular part of your day. When we experience mini successes like these, our brains release a small amount of dopamine, which motivates us to achieve more. This is why acknowledging all your small wins is so important. It will literally make you more productive!

10 WAYS TO FIND MOTIVATION WHEN YOU'RE TRULY STRUGGLING

- Look at your monthly goals (aka the Chalkboard Method™; see page 123) and find the easiest task. Take one step towards getting that task completed, even if it's just something small like ordering a book, reading a blog post or writing a plan of action.

- Take a cold shower. (Digital marketing coach Alice Benham swears by these!)
- Play 'Don't Stop Me Now' by Queen.
- Celebrate the small wins. Acknowledging the progress you've already made is a sure-fire way to boost your confidence and propel you onwards. Instead of writing a to-do list, write a DONE list. Make a note of everything you've done either that day or in relation to a specific project that's giving you the fear. Check each of them off with a big tick and bathe in your achievements.
- Douse yourself in your past successes. Psychologists say that positive feedback motivates us to keep working. Read over nice testimonials, messages or emails about work you've done in the past. Dig out your old school report card if you need to!
- Be clear on the benefit of what you're doing. Alexander Rothman's behavioural theory suggests that our brains are motivated when there is a payoff for our hard work: 'Decisions regarding behavioural initiation are predicted to depend on favourable expectations regarding future outcomes, whereas decisions regarding behavioural maintenance are predicted to depend on perceived satisfaction with received outcomes.[64] Basically, what are the long- and/or short-term benefits of the task at hand? If you focus on them, maybe even visualise them, it should get easier.
- Declare a fresh start. Remember how motivated you were at the start of the year to smash your goals? That feeling wasn't imagined, and it can be recreated. A

scientific study by the Wharton School of Business found that motivation increases after temporal landmarks (e.g. New Year, birthday, new semester, holiday), so it stands to reason that when we assign these fresh starts to a particular day, our motivation will increase. The study suggests that this process can 'relegate past imperfections to a previous period, induce people to take a big-picture view of their lives, and thus motivate aspirational behaviors'.[65]

- Watch the *Rocky* montage (or play the song from the movie).
- If you've got a financial goal in mind, write that figure on a piece of paper, pin it above your desk and make a note on it every time you get a step closer to achieving it.
- Text that one friend who takes pleasure in dishing out 'tough love' and ask for a pep talk.

ONLINE TOOLS FOR PRODUCTIVITY

GOOGLE FORMS
If you find introductory meetings take up a lot of your time, then consider creating a Google Form for prospective clients to complete which will give you all the details you need without the time required to have an initial phone call or meeting.

CALENDLY
To avoid the hours wasted playing email tennis with people, use Calendly to share available appointments with people

and they can select the time that works for them. I don't have enough meetings to use this myself, but I've booked meetings with other people who do use it and it's excellent.

MAILCHIMP

If you're building an email list then having an email marketing platform will help. You can link sign-up forms to your website so that when people sign up to your mailing list they get an automatic email. You can customise this to say whatever you want, point them to your socials, a blog post, or deliver them a free piece of content like an eBook or checklist. You can create separate lists, too, which is good for sending specific content to different audiences.

SOCIAL MEDIA SCHEDULER

If you find yourself throwing together social media posts on an ad-hoc basis without any planning, you might benefit from using a scheduling tool. There are several available, such as Buffer, Hootsuite, Later and CoSchedule. They allow you to draft posts, schedule for any time of the day and post automatically. In a few hours you can schedule a week's worth of content, but bear in mind that growth and engagement only occur when you actively use your platforms.

DESIGN TEMPLATES

I have to give a shout-out to all the amazing design templates available on Canva. The simplified graphic design website has an intuitive, drag-and-drop system that makes creating social media graphics, flyers, business cards and media kits ridiculously easy. The presentation templates are particularly good and have saved me hours of time creating slides for the many speaking gigs I've done over the past few years.

MONDAY.COM

If you're working on a project that involves collaborating with others, then Monday.com might work for you. I currently use it to plan social media posts for a client. It's essentially like a notice board where you can post tasks and leave comments on each one. You can label tasks, assign them to people, colour-code items and highlight when things are done or need attention. I was sceptical at first, but it's one of my favourite tools at the minute because it's very visuals-focused and it's super satisfying to label things as 'completed' once you're done.

OUTSOURCING

Shedding the responsibility of managing a team was one of the happiest moments of my life. I climbed the ladder in the catering industry because it was the only way to earn above minimum wage. I had no urge (or real ability) to be accountable for other people and it weighed heavily on me. I wanted my team to be great but I wasn't skilled at making that happen. I couldn't make people be good employees and it reflected on me as a manager. Being a perfectionist, of course, that really started to eat away at me. Moving into freelancing has had many plus points, but being accountable for my own actions, and no one else's, is definitely one aspect that keeps me working hard.

For that reason, I'm honestly reluctant to outsource my tasks to anyone else. Control freak? Quite possibly. But I also don't relish the idea of managing another person. I know lots of freelancers who have seen their businesses grow strong as a result of hiring others to help with the day-to-day tasks.

Take Vix Meldrew for instance, who runs a membership site for creatives called Grow & Glow. She was determined to focus on the creative parts of her business and delegate admin tasks to a virtual assistant. When I asked the reasoning behind this, she said:

> I didn't leave my career in teaching working 60–70 hours a week to do the same in my own business. I want to work as little as possible and that has always been my driving goal. There are lots of tasks I dread and I thought, I could spend £100 a month on ASOS or Deliveroo, or I could spend that on paying someone to do the jobs I hate so that I can focus on the things I do like. I just reprioritised where my money goes.

There is so much work that comes with being freelance, it's easy to feel overwhelmed with everything to the point where it actually stops you from moving forward.

Are you spending a day chasing invoices every month when you could be using that time to earn money doing creative work? If so, it may make financial sense to outsource the invoice-chasing to an assistant so that you can leave your schedule free to work on tasks that generate a higher income.

Hiring a virtual assistant can also help you with personal tasks that might be creeping into your work life, such as making appointments or buying gifts. It might even help you to hire a cleaner one day a month to keep your home spic and span.

Remember that outsourcing doesn't need to be a regular commitment; you can hire another freelancer on an ad-hoc basis and see how it goes. I've outsourced technical work and press outreach on a project-by-project basis and found it incredibly helpful.

KNOWING WHEN TO STOP

I'm a bit of a productivity nerd. I like figuring out sneaky
little ways to get more done and feel better as I do it, but,
like everyone, I have a limit. There comes a point where I
realise that no perfectly timed iced coffee or afternoon nap is
going to give me the jolt of energy I need to see me through
the day.

There comes a point when I'm buzzing with the wrong
kind of energy, nerves and anxiety, when I'm so tired and
yet I cannot sleep. The alarm goes off in the morning and I
think to myself, *Why did I choose this way of working? I wish I was
in regular employment so that I could phone in sick.* On those days,
productivity hacks are useless. On those days, we need other
solutions – ones that remind us that it's okay to be human and
slow down and say enough is enough.

The difference between pushing yourself for growth and
pushing yourself off the edge is a distinction that I struggle
with. I often don't realise I've gone over the edge until it's
too late and then I have to clamber my way back up the
mountain. I think this stems from the story that many of us
have been told, the one that tells us the show must go on at
all costs. The reality — as I'll explain in the final part of this
book — is that the show can and sometimes must, stop.

CHECKLIST

- Work to develop a routine that works for *you*.
- If you hate routine, make small promises to yourself that you'll aim to keep every day.
- Remove potential distractions.
- Keep a journal to identity your finest hour – then supercharge it.
- Consider outsourcing.
- Learn to prioritise.
- Know when to stop.

PART FOUR

THE SHOW MUST GO ON – RIGHT?

Mental health plays a key part in every business decision I make. I know that when my wellbeing starts to suffer, my capacity for work goes down the pan. I've been officially diagnosed with depression and anxiety, but that doesn't mean that you should skip this section if you haven't got a mental illness. Everyone has mental health (yep, even freelancers) and you should take it seriously. As the boss, it's your responsibility to take care of your one and only employee. Without them, you're in trouble.

In the final section of this book I've highlighted some of the negative emotions that tend to crop up for freelancers, and provided you with some tools that could help you manage them. I've also dedicated an entire chapter to something that many freelancers never think about: time off. I'm certainly not the poster gal for taking regular holidays, but I do see the value in them and I'm determined to get better at practising what I preach. As well as recreational time off, I also talk about emergency time off. The kind that you need when burnout creeps up on you or anxiety makes work impossible. I understand that these are circumstances that most freelancers don't want to contemplate, but having a plan in place for those unpredictable moments will give you the confidence to ride out the storm.

CHAPTER 19

MAINTAINING YOUR MENTAL HEALTH

This chapter is about the subject I hold close to my anxiously palpitating heart. Mental health. If I'm being real though, every single chapter in this book has some element of mental health because your happiness is affected by how you choose to run your business. Whether it's the way you present yourself on social media, how you pick which clients to work with, the monetary value you put on your services or what kind of diary you use to organise your days – the way you behave, the habits you form and the decisions you make all have the potential to negatively or positively impact your mental wellbeing.

Writing about mental health means that I've interviewed a lot of mental health professionals in my time – life hack: free therapy! – and I've done a lot of experimenting to find out what works for me in terms of maintaining a healthy mind. I've gleaned so many valuable tips that I've personally tried and tested against the struggles that come with living the OOO life.

Although I've been officially diagnosed with depression and anxiety and I speak from that experience, I urge every freelancer to prioritise their wellbeing from the word go. You don't have to wait until you reach crisis point to start taking care of yourself. Trust me, it's a very inefficient way of doing things. Without an annoying boss to check in on you now and again, it's your responsibility to create a work environment and healthy habits that keep you on an even keel.

MY STORY

On the day my first book was published I didn't know how to act. I had plenty of work to do but on Publication Day – the day that I had never dared to dream would actually exist – it seemed more fitting to mark the occasion. Friends sent flowers. My publisher sent me cupcakes with little edible paper images of my book cover pushed on the icing. I couldn't bear to eat them. I threw myself a mini celebration at lunchtime by inviting a few mates out for cider and pizza because it felt weird to sit at home in my work pyjamas.

When I got back home in the afternoon I felt out of place. After spending the previous ten months writing, editing and anticipating the release of my book, I had a gaping hole in my life now that it no longer needed to be created. I assumed that the gap would be filled by the printed book, an idea that had now become a physical entity, available for the world to consume. This was what I wanted.

But on Publication Day I didn't feel how I thought I would. I felt... empty. I decided to fill that void the only way I knew how. I wrote the proposal for this book. I know, pretty crazy right? After working long hours, writing in every spare minute I had, and cursing myself for ever agreeing to write my memoir, I came to the conclusion that I should probably repeat the process if I ever wanted to feel anything ever again. My yearly subscription to self-doubt and criticism has ended? This won't do! Sign me up for more please! I'll take a lifetime membership!

I wrote a very brief proposal on the day my book was published. I was ready to send it that day, but I thought that my editor would think me certifiably crazy (the first book already proved that, so it shouldn't really have been an issue), so I waited and sent it the next day. I patiently waited twenty-four hours in the hope that I would be seen as organised and enthusiastic, not desperately seeking validation.

But therein lies the truth. I need work to validate me. There you go. I've said it. I need exciting emails, challenging projects, scary meetings and big dreams. These are the things that make me feel like I'm doing something. And let me be frank, I don't think that this is a good thing.

Don't you think that after a year of working to find the most articulate way to tell a story based on the darkest moments of my life, I should have had a rest? Given myself some time to recover from the emotional sickness bug that is memoir writing? A few months to just enjoy being a published author without the self-induced pressure of doing it all again?

I do. I think I should have had a rest.

Instead, I pushed on relentlessly and secured a second contract because it's what us creative folks do. We chase any chance we get to do the thing we want to do. I acknowledge that we quite often do things that we know are against our best interests, and it's not big and it's not clever. I'm not going to act like I have my sh*t together mentally, because you can google my name and read all the articles I've written about feeling like an imposter, losing my rag over the tiniest of things and drinking on my medication. I'm only human, but I am trying to get better, and that's why I've dedicated a large portion of this book to talking about the importance of managing your mental health when you also manage your own workload.

I'm not perfect, but that's why we need this chapter. *No one* is perfect.

NEGATIVE EMOTIONS

The autonomy that comes with Being Your Own Boss (BYOB) is a double-edged sword. Instead of waiting for someone else to give you a pay rise, you can essentially implement one yourself if you have customers who are willing to pay you that amount. There are no forms to fill out in order to request a holiday. No dress code. No boring team meetings.

But alongside all those moments where you can't control your elation at the fact that this is your job, there are many, many moments filled with complicated emotions that can be hard to digest. I call this the BYOB pool of self-loathing. It's a deep and murky sinkhole that feels overwhelming and it's swirling with emotions that feed off each other, making it difficult to find your way out.

ANXIETY
Having been diagnosed with generalised anxiety disorder, it should come as no surprise that this feeling creeps up on me regularly. And yet somehow, it can still take me by surprise. I feel it before networking events and public speaking gigs, which is only natural, but I often feel it when I'm sitting at my desk trying to concentrate, too. Every creak of a floorboard sounds like an intruder, every email seems to

have a passive-aggressive undertone and every job takes
longer as I obsess over the quality of my work. Sometimes
I wake up with anxiety and can't get out of bed because
I feel sick at the thought of my to-do list. Physically, it
results in muscle tension, stomach cramps and headaches.
Mentally, I can't switch off at night and I lie awake
exhausted and full of worry.

GUILT

Every freelancer I know feels guilt like a dull headache.
It's always lurking in the background no matter what you
do. When I finish my to-do list a few hours early I often
consider changing into my pyjamas and watching *Bridesmaids*
with a hot cuppa and a packet of Oreos, but guilt generally
persuades me otherwise. Guilt has stopped me from investing
in training courses, buying books and upgrading my train
journey to first class. It has stopped me from taking time off
when I go home for Christmas and stopped me from staying
in bed when I'm dying with the flu.

FEAR

This feeling normally comes before negotiating rates with
a new client or trying to raise my prices with someone I
already work with. It also crops up when working with
people I really admire. What if they think I'm an idiot/my
work is awful/I have limp hair?

LONELINESS

God, I miss being able to talk to colleagues about the most
banal subjects. One day when I was working in the flat I had
to catch a butterfly that had just woken up from hibernation
and set it free. Had that happened in an office with someone

else present, I know it would have bonded us for life (catching a groggy little beast with wings is much harder than you might think), but I had to do it alone. Now it's just a story I tell at parties, that no one finds impressive.

LOW SELF-ESTEEM
Pitching feature ideas to magazines and websites is an excellent way to feel bad about yourself. You can have an idea come to you in the middle of the night, spend hours researching, find case studies, construct the most eloquent email, only to send it off to an editor and have it completely ignored. Even worse, you can get an email back that cuts you deep with three simple words: not for us. Depending on how much money I need, I can send up to ten emails of this nature daily, and a high percentage of them result in a big fat 'no'. For many freelancers, even those outside of the journalism industry, this scenario is common. With no boss to ask for feedback and no colleagues to sound off to, it's no wonder that this feeling of rejection can ruminate and fester into a sense that you're not good enough.

SHAME
Working independently comes with a sense of pride, one which many of us feel is lost as soon as we need to ask for support. I know that asking my clients for the things I need to get my job done often feels like I'm not a good problem-solver. I also get clients asking me to help with tasks that are outside my experience. Instead of saying, 'No, Sarah, I don't know how to write a Facebook ad', I find myself too ashamed to admit the truth. Weeks later I'm awake till 5 am reading blog posts trying to train myself to master a skill that

I don't even want. Why? The shame! And of course there's
the shame of asking to be paid, or, even worse, asking to
be paid more (see page 225). I'm working hard on this one
because I know that it will have a tangible impact on my
bank balance when I shed the embarrassment around asking
for money.

COMPARISON

You don't need me to tell you that comparing yourself to
people on the internet is bad for your mental health (the
global creative director of Facebook said that the average
person scrolls through 300ft of social media content every
day?[66] WTF), but for freelancers I think it's particularly rife,
because we are less likely to have a structure in place by
which to measure our own success. There are no personal
development programmes or company-wide targets that are
celebrated by teams. When I get my head down and focus
on my own goals, I tend to forget what everyone else is up to,
but as soon as I look up (and start scrolling) I suddenly feel
inadequate. The strangest part is that I often feel envious of
things that I don't even want. I certainly don't want to be
the face of Colgate toothpaste, but if I see a pretty blogger
doing an #AD, then you can bet your bottom dollar I'll be
comparing myself to her and her glistening smile.

WHY NEGATIVE EMOTIONS ARE HELPFUL

The BYOB pool of self-loathing is a place we all visit from
time to time and it's not necessarily a bad thing. I mean of
course you don't want to be drowning in it 24/7, but I think

that we can all learn a lesson or two by simply dipping our toes in from time to time.

Emotions are just signals, and it's how we react to those signals that can often cause trouble. Take the emotion of fear for example. You may feel an intense burst of fear when you hear a car speeding as you walk down the street, but this feeling signals you to step away from the kerb to an area of safety. This is an excellent response and one that has probably saved your life on a number of occasions. Let's look at another example. Say you're waiting on payment for a job you invoiced a month ago. You want to send an email to chase up the payment but you have a fear that if you do so, your client will be annoyed, and this could affect your working relationship going forward. So, instead of chasing the work, you wait, and you worry. This worry seeps into your everyday life and affects your mood and your sleep pattern. Eventually this turns to anger and a week later you send an email *demanding* payment. Do you see how fear itself didn't cause this outcome? It's how we *react* to emotions that can have the biggest impact.

This is why I believe that *feeling* negative emotions is so important to maintaining good mental health. Being exposed to small amounts of stress is actually good for us. A multi-year study conducted by UCLA found that people who experience moderate levels of trauma displayed better mental health than those who experience none at all. It seems that working through negative emotions can foster resilience and help people feel less distressed and have fewer post-traumatic stress symptoms, and higher life satisfaction over time than those without negative life events.[67] Perhaps more importantly, those who had lived through moderate adversity were least affected by more recent stressors. The study concluded that, 'in moderation, whatever does not kill us may indeed make us stronger.'[68]

TIP: Don't back away from negative emotions. Instead, try writing a letter to yourself explaining how you feel and what has led to this moment. You'll be amazed at the clarity that comes from writing it all down.

TOXIC POSITIVITY

To give a wider context to this idea, I think it's worth briefly touching on something known as toxic positivity. This is a concept that I've always been aware of but without realising it actually had a name until a few years ago. I find it's best explained in reference to a quote that regularly does the rounds on social media, and that's the phrase 'Good vibes only'. You've no doubt scrolled past this online or maybe even liked it or shared it yourself.

While the quote itself isn't necessarily harmful, it sums up the idea of toxic positivity because, at its core, it communicates the idea that only positive feelings (or vibes) should be felt in order to achieve a sense of happiness. It suggests that we can (and should) choose to adopt a certain sunny disposition and reject any negative feelings that come our way.

The problem with this is that by refusing to experience negative emotions, we deny ourselves the opportunity to build resilience, as discussed in relation to the UCLA study. And so when increasingly intense, unavoidable negative emotions come along in the future, we are less able to deal with them in a healthy way.

So, as I say, I certainly don't advise diving head first into the BYOB pool of self-loathing, but I would argue that dipping your toe in isn't necessarily all bad. For example, comparing yourself to other people feels pretty gross, but if you take a step back it can be a signal that you're feeling inadequate in some area of your life. I often get jealous when I learn how much money other freelancers make. It can be easy to use that as a reason to feel sorry for myself, but when I take a look at my own behaviours I realise that the jealousy is really just a signal that highlights the fact that I need to raise my prices and start looking for clients who value my work. When you can turn that little dip in the pool into positive action, you avoid full-on submersion, and that, my friends, is progress.

However, that doesn't mean that every negative emotion can be dealt with swiftly and without consequence. And while those in regular employment often get access to the support of colleagues and professional counselling services, it can be much harder for us freelancers to notice and act upon the symptoms of serious mental illness. Before we talk about mental illness, though, there is one major red flag that I think every freelancer should be aware of, and that is burnout.

BURNOUT

The problem with most of the emotions we find in the pool of self-loathing is that they force you to work harder. The fear of having no money means that you will take on extra jobs that you don't really have the time for. Low self-esteem means that you don't have the confidence to set healthy boundaries with clients and so you answer emails at midnight and go to bed with a knot in your stomach which means you don't get enough sleep. You compare yourself to a seemingly successful sibling/friend/stranger on the internet and decide that the route to fulfilment looks like hard work and not a lot else. You push harder, work longer and get results. But at what cost?

Burnout showed up for me after a five-year stint in catering management. I was hell bent on climbing the career ladder but I didn't really know where I was going, or why. I guess maybe I hoped there would be a nice view from the top? It turns out I just got very sick.

In 2019, the World Health Organization officially classified burnout as 'a syndrome conceptualized as resulting from chronic workplace stress that has not been successfully managed'. The WHO also stipulated three major symptoms that characterise burnout in patients. They are:

- feelings of energy depletion or exhaustion;
- increased mental distance from one's job, or feelings of negativism or cynicism related to one's job; and
- reduced professional efficacy.[69]

Having grown up in a world where the word burnout could easily have been exchanged for terms like 'lazy' or 'under the weather', I'm relieved that medical professionals have now acknowledged the seriousness of the condition. The thing I've come to learn is that burnout exists on a sliding scale and many of the symptoms can overlap with mental illnesses. Left untreated, it can escalate. If you're lucky, the very early signs of burnout can be dealt with over a long weekend in the same way you would treat food poisoning. Sleep. Hydrate. Watch everything on Netflix. Other cases of burnout are so severe that they can lead to long-term mental illness, and this is why as a freelancer you need to be able to recognise the symptoms of burnout and take them seriously when they appear.

Burnout is something that you *can* work to overcome.

COMMON SYMPTOMS OF BURNOUT INCLUDE:

- Physical and mental exhaustion
- Indecisiveness
- Insomnia
- Increase in physical illness (colds, viruses, etc.)
- Irritability
- Feeling overly emotional
- Forgetfulness
- Lack of focus
- Sense of dread or hopelessness

WHAT TO DO IF YOU EXPERIENCE BURNOUT

Having dealt with burnout repeatedly myself, I find it hard to pinpoint exactly how I recovered from it in the first instance – partially because I didn't realise that I was suffering from burnout at the time and partially because I was actually treating the symptoms of depression above all else. But since becoming a freelancer I've caught myself teetering on the edge of burnout multiple times and sunk right into it on a few occasions too. And yet here I sit telling the tale, because burnout is something that you *can* work to overcome.

In an article published on Psychology Today, Sherrie Bourg Carter Psy.D writes,

The good news is that burnout is not a terminal condition. Although it certainly requires a change in lifestyle, once burnout is recognised and attended to, it can become a positive force in your life, a chance to rediscover yourself and shine brightly once again.

First things first, if you're exhibiting any of the symptoms in the box on the previous page, go and see a doctor. I'm not a GP, so please, for the love of god, use anything I say here as a tasty little side dish to complement the meat and two veg which is **actual medical advice**.

DEALING WITH BURNOUT

- Check your finances. Do you have a buffer fund? If so, can you afford to take some time off to recover?
- Write down all the things that are causing you stress. Now, next to each one write down some ideas about how you can make these less stressful. (For example, at the moment writing this book is quite stressful. I can make this less so by asking for an extension on the deadline, getting help transcribing interviews and by breaking the word count into manageable chunks.)
- Out of all the stressful things on your list, cross off anything that is non-essential. This might mean letting some people down, but f*ck it, your health comes first.
- Write down a list of all the things that make you feel relaxed. Now, be honest, are you really making time for these things? Take action to prioritise these activities on a daily basis by setting a reminder or writing them in your schedule. Think of them as a form of medication that you need to take in order to get better.
- Be truthful with your clients. Tell them that you're taking a bit of time off because you're not feeling well but that as soon as you're feeling better you can't wait to work with them again. They will appreciate your honesty.
- Be sensible. Limit your booze, get outside once a day, eat a vegetable now and again and, of course, stay hydrated.

- Rest. I mean, *really* rest.
- Stop saying yes to stuff you hate.
- Prioritise the activities that feed your soul, like laughing with friends and walking on the beach. These acts are truly healing in the greatest sense of the word.

In addition to these practical tips, I highly recommend trying something totally radical. Try to forgive yourself. Sixty per cent of freelancers feel that poor mental health, stress or anxiety has at some point had a negative impact on their ability to work,[70] so find comfort in the fact that there are quite a lot of other people feeling less than tickety-boo about how they handle their sh*t. It doesn't mean that you're at the end of the road or that you're a bad freelancer; you're just going through a tough time that (science has proved) will more than likely make you stronger in the long run. Yay!

BUILDING YOUR OWN MENTAL HEALTH TOOLKIT

Since being diagnosed with depression and anxiety I've had to navigate life while trying to control my symptoms. I've tried lots of different "solutions", from meditation to exercise, and what I've learnt is that there isn't one antidote for my mental health ailments. It changes depending on my mood, location, time of the month and energy levels.

Imagine your coping mechanism is running. That's great. Neurologists say that running can mitigate the negative impacts of chronic stress.[71] But what happens when you're on a high-pressure business trip and your schedule is too busy to fit in exercise? Or when you fracture your ankle and have to spend weeks working from bed? You still experience the stress, but you can't access your fail-safe tool for working through it. This is exactly why you need to have a bag full of tricks that you can delve into to keep your brain working *for* you instead of against you.

WHO'S ON YOUR TEAM?

While we should all take ownership of our wellbeing and draw on tools that make us feel empowered to make change, there's no denying the benefit of a good support network. This means letting people in, not pushing them away. The next time your mum offers to make you a batch of lasagne for your freezer, don't belittle her for insinuating you're regressing to childhood. The fact is we all need a back-up plan for when we can't adult, and if pre-made cheesy pasta isn't a perfectly formed back-up plan then I don't know what is. As well as your adorable mum, here are a few other people who might help as part of your support network:

YOUR BIGGEST CHEERLEADER

The person who tags you in memes on the daily about jokes you made fifteen years ago, buys everything you sell, promotes your business to everyone she meets and sends you a bunch of flowers when you achieve anything, even if it's something that no one else understands like getting a guest appearance on a super-niche podcast.

THE MOTHER FIGURE

In lieu of a lasagne-making mother, this person is always on hand to fill your belly with homemade food and endless cups of tea. She'll drop everything when you need her and she'll always bring biscuits.

THE TRUTH TELLER

She'll compassionately tell you what you need to hear without being a total b*tch. Want feedback on your branding? She'll tell you how it is. Need someone to check the spelling on your CV? She's got your back. Want someone to make sure you don't order tequila shots at 3 am? She'll hand you a bottle of water and take you to the nearest kebab shop to sober up.

THE FREELANCER TWIN

The one who is also waiting on overdue invoices and knows all the answers to your tax-related questions. She too works at home and is the only one of your mates who is free to listen to a ten-minute voice note on a Tuesday morning which goes into detail about why Comic Sans needs to go into Room 101. She's also your partner in crime for cheeky afternoons at the pub and cheap spa days.

MR MOTIVATOR

This guy gives you a pep in your step, a pat on the back, and after every interaction you walk away feeling like you've just drunk a can of Red Bull. A life-giver and true sparkly person. Self-doubt doesn't stand a chance when Mr Motivator is around.

SLEEP

I've spent most of my life trying to get up earlier. When I was at school I would shower in the evenings to get an extra thirty minutes in bed. When I was in a job I would skip breakfast for the same reason. I always packed my gym bag the night before a 6 am sweat sesh, but every single time concocted some reason to hit snooze on the alarm instead. The truth is I'm someone who needs a lot of sleep. I'm not a morning person and if I haven't had at least six hours (closer to ten TBH) then I'm not an afternoon person either. The whole day is a write-off. I always attributed my need for mammoth sleep sessions to nothing other than pure laziness, but the truth is that everyone's sleep requirements are different.

Sleep is as important to good health as eating, drinking and breathing. Studies have even found long-term sleep deprivation is linked to problems with eyesight, speech and memory. Multiple days of no sleep whatsoever can even cause you to hallucinate.

I won't patronise you with any further tips on how to get a better night's sleep. The basics read like this:

- Minimise caffeine
- Reduce screen time
- Take a warm bath
- Meditate
- Go bed at the same time every night
- Sleep in a cool room
- Get up at roughly the same time every morning

Unless you have full-on insomnia, getting enough sleep should be relatively simple. But for freelancers, it sometimes falls to the bottom of the priority list. Sitting at our desks always seems like a better use of our time than lying in bed, but try your best to shift the guilt that comes with getting enough shut-eye. The time you spend sleeping will allow your brain to recover and regenerate, consolidate memory and allow you to learn and function when you are awake. It's literally an investment in your future health as well as your productivity levels.

EXERCISE

I have an interesting relationship with fitness. When I was growing up I did no exercise. When I was at university I did even less. But when I was diagnosed with depression and anxiety I started going to fitness classes every day. Partly because I heard it is good for mental health, but mostly to gain some sense of control over my life because I was off work with zero structure to speak of. Since then I've had phases in my life where I've been dangerously obsessed with exercise and losing weight. At other times I've avoided the gym for months on end. But one thing has always been true. Moving my body has a tangible impact on my wellbeing. Assuming that I don't start going for three hours a day (which I was at one stage, and became so fanatical that I even trained to become a fitness instructor), then I know that exercise needs to be a key part of my mental health.

As discussed throughout this book, freelancers are likely to experience feelings of anxiety. Exercise is such an under-utilised tool for this occupational hazard. According to an article on the Harvard Health Publishing website, taking part in exercise:

- Diverts you from the thing you are anxious about
- Decreases muscle tension, lowering the body's contribution to feeling anxious

- Changes brain chemistry, increasing the availability of important anti-anxiety neurochemicals, including serotonin, gamma aminobutyric acid, brain-derived neurotrophic factor and endocannabinoids
- Activates frontal regions of the brain responsible for executive function, which helps control the amygdala, the part that reacts to real or imagined threats to our survival

In addition, exercising regularly builds up resources that bolster resilience against stormy emotions.[72] Remember the BYOB pool of self-loathing we spoke about earlier? Physical exercise is a way to make yourself stronger, ready to deal with all the icky feelings of guilt, shame and comparison.

This rings true for me in a number of ways. Social anxiety is always lurking in the background, but every week I get myself out of the house and I walk into a sweaty exercise studio full of strangers and I do an aerobics class. I high-five the women next to me. Sometimes we even get into pairs and have to look each other in the eye as we do burpees. It's the most awkward thing, but I do it and l have fun. More importantly, though, I prove to myself that I can do things that feel scary.

I interviewed Poorna Bell, journalist and author of *In Search of Silence*, who spoke to me about her relationship with powerlifting. She found that the positive impact of getting physically stronger – by lifting weights and increasing that weight over time – trickled through to her freelance life too, especially at times when work wasn't going as well as planned:

> *That sense of achievement and working towards something in the gym makes you feel that your life is progressing even if it's not progressing in other areas. It gives you more confidence in work*

meetings. With freelancing it can feel like you have to get your
self-worth internally because it's not going to come from a manager,
and I found that powerlifting was a very good way to generate that.
It also makes you very self-sufficient because you can actually lift
heavy things and move them around. That sounds ridiculous but
it's true!

TIP: Exercise doesn't need to be lifting weights and
running marathons. Take a walk around the block or do a
Pilates video on YouTube – whatever feels good to you.

SOCIALISING

It's also worth mentioning that exercising in a group setting
can kill several birds with one stone. You can get all the
mood-boosting, anxiety-shifting, resilience-building benefits
and tackle the isolation problem that I spoke about earlier in
this book. (Refer back to Chapter 15 for advice on building
support networking without the exercise element mentioned
here.) One study found that older adults who took part in
a 'walk and talk' project felt more motivated to socialise,
experienced reduced feelings of loneliness and felt a sense of
belonging as a result.[73]

Poorna has similar feelings in relation to her own fitness
journey. The reason she started weight lifting in the first place
was because it was a solitary activity, but her personal trainer
kindly nudged her into training, eating and socialising with a
team. Initially, she was not on board.

'I couldn't think of anything worse!' she tells me. 'But I learnt there's something really valuable about pushing yourself out of your comfort zone because I was initially very shy about getting to know them but then incrementally once you put in the time you form quite solid relationships.'

There was also the added benefit of building her social circle:

'I live on my own, I work from home and I've chosen an area without any friends or family nearby. It wasn't until I found this team of people nearby that I realised if I need help there are people nearby. Some of them are even freelancers, so it's really nice to have people to hang around with at odd times of the day and that's really filled a gap that I didn't realise I was missing.'

NUTRITION

Remember that wee woman who took over our screens in the year 2004, examining human poop on the TV show *You Are What You Eat*? Gillian McKeith may not have said anything of much value since her qualifications were publicly questioned (a journalist famously bought the same diploma for his dead cat Hettie[74]), but think of the name of her show merely as a jumping-off point for this section in which I urge you, at the very least, to cast a thoughtful eye over the food you put in your mouth.

I know it's patronising to hear that your mood fluctuations could be linked to the number of donuts you've eaten in the past week, but it's worth remembering that 95% of the serotonin in your body is secreted in your gut.[75] Ensuring that your gut is functioning normally, then, is probably a good idea, because serotonin is believed to 'help regulate mood and social behaviour, appetite and digestion, sleep, memory, and sexual desire and function'.[76]

I'm no expert (although, to be fair, neither was Gillian), but I have spent a number of years playing trial and error with lots of different lifestyle changes to see how they impact my mental health. Caffeine, in my case, is best enjoyed in small doses, otherwise it gets my heart racing and triggers anxiety attacks. Sugar does the same. I remember once throwing caution to the wind and eating a Nutella crepe for lunch, feeling high on sugar for an hour and then crashing so hard and so fast that I had to take to my bed for a nap at 2 pm. The nature of freelancing means that afternoon naps are logistically possible (and an undeniable perk), but believe me, you won't get much done if you need one every time you eat a pancake.

So, in lieu of my own knowledge on the subject, I've roped in my friend Rachael Watson. She's a nutritionist with years of experience training clients one-to-one and delivering online training, as well as recently taking up a role with the NHS. You can find out more about her at ditchthedietacademy.com. Although I trust her fully, this too shouldn't be taken instead of medical advice; it should, however, give you – yes, I'm going to say it – some food for thought.

EATING WELL FOR YOUR MIND, BY RACHAEL WATSON

Ever heard someone say, 'The way to my happiness is through my stomach'?

Well, that has a lot more meaning to it than it would appear on the surface. In recent years, there has been extensive and ongoing research into the connection between what we eat and the way our brains and bodies process emotion – in particular, the way we handle difficult or negative emotions.

The most notable was a landmark study concluded in 2017 (the 'SMILES' trial) which showed that participants who ate a Mediterranean-style diet (eating a wide variety of vegetables, fruits, legumes, oily fish and healthy fats like olive oil) for twelve weeks were much more likely to improve their mood than those who followed a placebo diet. This is due to an increase in the number and variety of healthy gut bacteria, which was promoted by the foods commonly eaten as part of a Mediterranean-style diet.

So, does that mean we should all jump on the next flight to Spain or Italy? If that's a bit of a stretch for you, there are some really simple and easy things you can do at home to support your mental health when it comes to your diet. These are written by me, a decade-long veteran of anxiety and depression, who is sitting on a stool across from you, not on a pedestal above you looking down. I understand how challenging it can be to carry out the most basic of tasks when you are feeling low, so I'll keep these simple and effective. Choose the easy ones on bad days, and challenge yourself with the more demanding ones when you're feeling better.

1   **Hydrate with water.** It sounds simple, but I know how tempting it is to fuel your morning with caffeine

and end your day with alcohol when you're feeling low. Aim for 6–8 glasses of water every single day, starting first thing in the morning. You could start by swapping just one of your daily coffees for a glass of water instead, or even herbal tea.

2   **Buy some healthy, balanced ready meals and put them in the freezer.** This kinda goes hand in hand with #4, but is even easier if you're struggling to find energy to cook something. It's important to be prepared.

3   **Increase the colour in your day.** I'm not talking about colouring in (though I do love that too), I'm talking about your plate. Each time you make a meal, have a look at it and check how colourful it is. At the end of each week, see if you can manage to eat at least two things from each colour of the rainbow. This will ensure you're getting a wide range of vitamins and minerals – which is essential for maintaining good mental health.

4   **Be prepared.** On days and weeks where you're feeling good, prepare for days when you might not feel so good. Plan some healthy meals and pack some away in the freezer. Then you'll always have something nutritious to eat that requires nothing more than 4–5 minutes in the microwave.

5   **Include a portion of healthy fats at every meal.** Eating healthy fats is important because some crucial micronutrients can't be absorbed and used by the body to keep you healthy without fat to

help transport them. Your portion of healthy fat at each meal should be about the size of your thumb. Healthy fats can be found in foods like nuts, seeds, avocado, dark chocolate and oils like extra virgin olive oil.

6 **Increase the fibre content of your meals** by considering lowering your meat intake and introducing more foods like beans and pulses. The probiotics in your gut (good bacteria) feed on these fibres and multiply. Eating a variety of different fibres will increase the variety of good bacteria in your gut, which has been linked to improved mood and lowered risk and symptoms of depression.

7 **Slow down!** You're self-employed and you probably wear ten different hats every single day – I get it, you're BUSY. However, you absolutely must make time to eat. By this, I mean sit down, at a table (without your laptop), and focus on eating the meal that you've taken time to prepare. Chew your food properly before you swallow it. I know this sounds absolutely ludicrous, but inhaling meals with one hand while typing with the other inhibits digestion, which can cause digestive discomfort. Proper digestion = happy gut bugs. Happy gut bugs = a healthier, happier mind.

8 I hate to be the party pooper, but **be mindful of your alcohol intake**. Yes, the Meds love their red wine, but try to be sensible, as alcohol is a well-known irritant of the gut, and we're trying to keep it as happy as

possible. Aim to stay under fourteen units per week for both men and women (this is equivalent to around seven medium-sized glasses of wine).

By taking care of your digestive system, you are automatically taking care of your mood. Not only will eating a diet rich in variety, colour and fibre promote good gut and mental health, it will also give you a great sense of self-worth, satisfaction and energy, which I think is so important when embarking upon a career as a freelancer.

GETTING OUTSIDE

If you're anything like me, you'll manage to convince yourself that certain things aren't important. Like ironing, drying the dishes (they're drip drying, okay?) or going outside, for example. The thing is, when you go to an external space to work (like an office or a shop), you have to leave the house. You have to go outside to get in your car, walk or get the train to be in a specific place to do your job. You automatically breathe fresh air and feel the weather on your skin without really thinking about it. But working from home means that unless you have an appointment or a dog to walk, going outside is entirely optional. It can seem counterproductive to go wandering around the park when you've got a website to design or emails to respond to, but prioritising being outside – even for just a short time – can go a long way to helping you maintain a healthy mind. Researchers from the University of Essex found that as little as five minutes of a 'green activity' such as walking, gardening, cycling or farming can boost mood and self-esteem.[77]

Working in front of a screen can often lead to that 'tired but wired' feeling. I know I've spent many a night lying awake, frustrated, desperately wishing sleep to come. Experts say that this horrible feeling is a sign that our nervous systems are in overdrive. The good news is that nature stimulates our parasympathetic nervous system, which is responsible for the 'rest and restore' areas of our brain, which helps us relax and get a good night's sleep.[78]

However you get outside is up to you. Incorporate it into your exercise routine, take your breaks out on your balcony, schedule meetings on your favourite park bench if you want to! When I have a call to check in with a client I often walk up to my local duck pond and take the call from there. As long as I don't need my laptop, I can speak from any location, so why not make it outdoors?

TIP: If you've made friends with other freelancers in your area, then why not organise a regular walk-and-talk meet-up? It's a good way to get outdoors but also have some interesting conversations.

MAKING TIME FOR CREATIVITY

Lots of freelancers work in creative roles – graphic design, copywriting, product development, branding. But there is a difference between being creative at work and being creative for your own mental health. Creativity at work is often hemmed in by guidelines set by the client. You might be doing a creative task but on a topic that doesn't excite you. You might create something you're incredibly proud of only to have the client say it's not what they want, leaving you feeling personally attacked and with a hell of a lot of work to do. For these reasons, finding a creative outlet which is just for fun can have a huge impact on your mental health. We all get days when we feel unmotivated, but being a freelancer means that you can potentially use those days as an excuse to do something else.

If you choose to do something creative instead of moping around, you might find that you get a massive mood boost as a result. A study of 658 university students in New Zealand found that people participating in creative activities felt more enthusiasm than usual the day after the activity.[79] This suggests there is an 'upward spiral' that comes with getting your creative on. In this study, Dr Tamlin Conner reported that participants who took part in daily creativity (e.g. poetry, writing, drawing, musical performance) began to exhibit higher levels of enthusiasm and flourishing. I know what you're thinking. You're thinking that I've made a stupid typo there, but the truth is that 'flourishing' is a 'psychological concept that can be described as increasing positive growth in oneself'. So what are you waiting for? Grab that paint brush and FLOURISH.

In addition, creativity has been known to help develop these skills:

- The ability to cope with stress
- Finding creative solutions to problems

- Finding ways to be mindful, to relax and enjoy the moment
- Feeling confident and trusting in ourselves
- Finding meaning in the world around us
- Knowing who we are
- Having hopes and goals in life, feeling useful

In conclusion, it would be crazy for you *not* to make creativity a part of your bag of tricks, because I bet you'll enjoy a bit of flourishing, and it will almost certainly benefit your mental health.

PROFESSIONAL HELP

When you've exhausted your bag of tricks and you still feel like utter crap, it's time to call in the big guns. This is one aspect of mental health maintenance that so many of us (myself included) never fully engage with. For many of us freelancers, success only feels real when achieved under the banner of self-sufficiency. We pride ourselves in being the lone wolf, a company of one, and while it's freeing to have the autonomy of freelancing, that doesn't mean that we don't need support.

I'll talk a bit more about getting professional help in the next chapter, but you shouldn't feel ashamed about going to the doctor or googling local therapists in a haze at 3 am. Sometimes the most crystal-clear moments appear in the wee hours, and if you're thinking about asking for help, the chances are you need it more than you're willing to admit.

TIP: Create your own 'wellness at work' scheme as though you are a CEO setting a mental health policy for your team. What would you want your employees to have in order to prioritise their wellbeing? Enforced lunch breaks? Daily walks? An early finish on a Friday? Draw up a list of strategies you can implement in your own home office going forward.

10 PRACTICAL WAYS TO MANAGE YOUR MENTAL HEALTH

1   Eat a varied diet filled with lots of colour and some healthy fats
2   Take a few hours to do something creative
3   SLEEP
4   Get outside
5   Move your body
6   Talk to people in real life
7   Set longer deadlines
8   Take time each month to plan, see the big picture
9   Increase your rates, and stop doing little tasks for your client without charging them
10 Ask a virtual assistant to do a few hours a week for you and see how it feels

CHECKLIST

- Recognise the negative emotions that come with freelancing
- Begin to understand the role they play (it's not healthy to be positive all the time!)
- Be aware of the symptoms of burnout
- Build your own mental health toolkit
- Sleep, socialise, exercise and eat well

CHAPTER 20

TAKING TIME OFF

You're probably looking at the title of this chapter and rolling your eyes. Time off? As a freelancer? Chance would be a fine thing! Yep, I hear you. I'm just as perplexed as you by the idea of downing tools and taking time off. I'm currently writing this chapter on Boxing Day, sitting in my dad's office at my parents' house, listening to my family watch *Home Alone 2* through the wall as I hammer out a few thousand words. I am livid. But you know what? Time off doesn't look the same for us freelancers as it does for everyone else. And you know what else? I could have taken today off if I had planned accordingly, but I'm still learning how to be a healthy freelancer, so please forgive me.

HOLIDAYS

Goal-setting is something that I – like most freelancers – get pretty excited about. I tend to be pretty ambitious, dreaming of pivotal career moments like doing a TED talk or having my memoir adapted into a movie (who would play me? Kirsten Dunst, obviously), but one thing I am awful

I think as
freelancers we
need to accept
that most of us
have a love affair
with work.

at planning for is a holiday. It just doesn't occur to me to schedule one in. You forget that in traditional employment paid holidays are a legal necessity, and I, personally, would never not use up my full entitlement. But, as a freelancer, holidays feel like such an unnecessary luxury.

Every few years my mum will ask if I want to go away for a beach holiday and I'll always jump at the chance, and when my brother emigrated to Australia I spent a year planning to go and visit him. But these wonderful getaways have been, gratefully so, thrust upon me by an external force. I really struggle to take the initiative when it comes to planning time off throughout the year, even if it's just for a staycation.

Here's the thing: I love my work. I complain about it regularly (it's healthy to vent, if you ask me), but I obsess over it in the most glorious way because I'm passionate about building a successful business. I think as freelancers we need to accept that most of us have a love affair with work. We really enjoy the graft, the struggle and the ownership and so letting go of that thing, even if it's just for a week, can give us separation anxiety. But in the same way that you have to let your crazy Labrador puppy stay home unattended for an hour while you run to the shop for toilet paper, you have to learn to step away from your business now and again. Yes, there may be a small amount of mess to clear up when you get back, but there will also be lessons learnt. And you will have toilet paper.

Here are a few red flags that signal you need some time off:

- Poor personal hygiene
- Weight loss/gain

- Problems sleeping or sleeping too much
- Exhaustion
- Constant irritability
- Palpitations
- Lack of motivation
- Brain fog
- No interest in things you normally enjoy
- Socially withdrawn

If you're checking a few of these off the list then take a good hard look at your schedule and see where you can logistically squeeze in a few days off. Getting a wee rest in before these symptoms escalate is the ultimate gift to yourself. Go on, you deserve it!

WHY YOU NEED A HOLIDAY

We all know that holidays are great for our health, but did you know that they are good for business too? In regular employment, when you're not performing at your best, the chances are this won't have a major impact on the business as a whole, but when you are self-employed you make up 100% of the workforce. While that might sound scary, it also means that you only need to worry about giving one person the best possible break in order to dramatically improve company morale. Time off can:

- Give you a better perspective on life
- Help you look at the bigger picture
- Spark creative ideas
- Increase your energy levels

- Improve productivity
- Help you cope with stress
- Boost your immune system
- Improve sleep

If you saw that list of benefits on the side of a pill bottle, would you take it? I know I would. That's how you need to think about time off: it's a form of medication that will improve your health and therefore your business as a whole.

THE PROBLEM WITH HOLIDAYS

In the UK, full-time workers are entitled to a minimum of twenty-eight days' paid annual leave, and yet IPSE research shows that the average freelancer takes just twenty-four days of holiday per year.[80] The majority of freelancers agree that time off improves their work-life balance, has a positive effect on relationships and eases feelings of stress and anxiety. But one in ten of us struggle to take a single day off in any given year. Even worse, four out of five freelancers[81] admit to working when they are on holiday, which kind of defeats the purpose, don't you think?

Well, it's tricky. In an ideal world, every holiday would involve complete relaxation. No thoughts about work, no bright ideas for future projects, no worrying about how your client got on at that big meeting. Just bottomless piña coladas and lots of staring thoughtfully at the horizon. It's a lovely picture, but I don't think it's always realistic to completely disconnect from your business, especially when you're just starting out.

I'm not saying you should crack open your laptop and get a full eight hours in from your sun lounger, but I don't necessarily think there's anything wrong with checking your emails halfway through the week to make sure that there are no major fires that need putting out. It can be really hard to forget about work when you're off, and often this turns into anxiety about what awaits you when you return. If you find this overwhelming, then you might feel better popping online to check that everything is okay. But that is something that should be *your* decision and no one else's, by which I mean as far as your clients are concerned, you are on holiday – and that means you're uncontactable.

> TIP: Give your clients plenty of warning that you're going to be taking a break and set a friendly out-of-office response that makes it crystal clear you are on holiday and will deal with any emails upon your return.

EMERGENCY TIME OFF

Jetting off for a week in Spain with your besties is one thing, but taking sick leave is an entirely different beast. With holidays, you have an extended period of time to mentally and financially prepare. You can set aside money, warn your clients and do extra work in the lead-up to make sure that everything is taken care of in your absence. But sickness and other events (e.g. mental illness, family drama, the death of someone close to you) come without warning and therefore require a little more forward planning.

HOW TO PLAN FOR EMERGENCY TIME OFF

- Start an online savings pot for unplanned time off. If you set aside £20 a week, you'll have £1,000 within a year.
- Test out some virtual assistants so that you feel confident delegating work to them in an emergency.
- Consider getting income protection insurance to help cover your outgoings if you are unable to work due to sickness.
- Practise different skills. Being off with a broken leg means you might have to stop working in a physical role for a while, but you could still make money via another avenue such as delivering online courses or copywriting.

WHEN TIME OFF FEELS IMPOSSIBLE

I'm not going to sit here and lie about my own ability to take time off. I am certifiably terrible, and I have no shame in admitting that to you and the rest of the world. I can plan for holidays and take the odd half-day here and there when I have the flu, but there have been several occasions in my freelance life when I've known full well that I'm making myself physically and mentally ill by continuing to work. I've cried at my desk while sending invoices. I've prioritised writing social media captions over personal hygiene. I've had a panic attack on a long-haul flight, slept it off and woken up with the need to write a blog post. I've refused to slow down and stop so many times. Not because I want to push on, but because there's just been so much work to do that it's felt impossible. Like a pipe dream.

I've realised that layering guilt about not slowing down on top of my feelings of mental exhaustion is pointless and messy. Sometimes – and this decision lies within your own personal circumstances – time off isn't always feasible.

As I've been writing this book, it's certainly felt this way. The first deadline coincided with the Christmas holidays and it triggered a major relapse for me, something that I should have been prepared for but I wasn't. I knew that I needed time off to rest and recalibrate but it didn't feel like an option because I wanted to push through and submit the first draft on time. Could I have pushed the deadline back a few weeks? Probably, but I felt like getting it out of the way was better than prolonging the agony. But as I waded through the last few weeks of writing, knowing that I should be taking time off, I did make some adjustments to my life. I knew I was screeching towards a head-on collision, but I tried to do some damage control to minimise the long-term ramifications of burning the midnight oil. I'm not saying that 'getting on with it' is the healthiest approach to managing ill health – absolutely not. But if, for whatever reason, you have to wait a few days or weeks before you take some time off, here are some tips to manage in the meantime:

- Take yourself off social media – literally, delete that sh*t.
- Reschedule all unnecessary meetings.
- Cancel all social events that will drain you.
- Make time for one or two social events that will energise you.
- Forgive yourself for not exercising and, instead, try to get outside once a day for fresh air.
- Take small breaks often.

- Call up your most understanding clients and explain the situation. Ask for extensions on any deadlines.
- Forgive yourself for not cooking every day. Instead, opt for the healthiest ready meals you can find. Biscuits aren't the enemy.
- Minimise caffeine even though it seems like madness.
- Try not to lean on booze to get you off to sleep. Try reading or meditation instead.
- Stay hydrated.
- Make time for the things you love. I promise you sixty minutes spent on your favourite hobby will give you a much-needed boost.
- Call in favours from loved ones to help you stay on top of life admin, whether it's making appointments, cleaning the house, taking the dog for a walk, etc.
- Set an autoresponder on your email to give people a realistic timeframe for when you'll get back to them. Alternatively, tell people you're out of the office, which will limit email distractions even more!

TIP: Guilt is an extremely common feeling for freelancers in relation to time off. Try imagining that you are the employer of a staff member who doesn't want to take time off because they feel they don't deserve it. What would you say to them? How would you ease their guilt? Can you see how the company benefits from employees who prioritise their own health and happiness?

CHECKLIST

- Take at least one proper holiday every year
- Start a savings fund for emergency time off
- Find a good virtual assistant that you can call on short notice
- Get income protection insurance

FINAL THOUGHTS

Congratulations, you made it to the end!

But now that the reading part is done, where does that leave us? You could close the book, slide it onto your bookshelf and let it gather dust. Forget about everything I've said, actively choose to ignore all of my well-researched advice and go about your day, and your life, never implementing any changes or embarking on your OOO dream. That's cool; it's a viable option and I'll only be slightly offended.

Seriously, though, I've tried to make this a balanced account of all that a foray into freelancing entails, so I'm more than prepared for it to put some of you off. It's a lot of work and it's not for everyone. If you've decided not to pursue freelancing then you're still entitled to feel proud AF because decision-making of any sort is to be commended. I respect that entirely, and I bid you adieu.

However, if you've found yourself feeling pangs of excitement while flicking through these pages or scribbled down new ideas in your notepad, then there's a good chance that freelancing is a world you should consider exploring further.

Maybe you're sick of rocking up to the office every Monday filled with anxiety. Maybe you've thought about freelancing before but never found the confidence to get going. Maybe you've dipped your toe in already and, for whatever reason, it didn't work out. Maybe you're twelve months in and you're treading water, wondering if it ever gets easier. Whatever stage of the journey you're at, I salute you. I also stand with you, in a tired, weary and slightly manic state of mind, because, my god, the OOO path certainly isn't the easiest one. Yep, prepare for things to get messy.

But nothing good ever came easy, did it? Achieving what you want in life is often just a case of working hard, never giving up and trying to enjoy the process. Hopefully, with everything you've learnt in these pages, you'll feel armed to make good decisions, find paying clients and take care of yourself along the way.

Now get that notepad and start making a plan. Your future is waiting.

ACKNOWLEDGEMENTS

First of all, thank you to Trigger Publishing for giving me the opportunity to write about a topic that is so close to my heart. Thanks to Kasim Mohammed for your enthusiasm with getting this project started and for your endless encouragement ever since. Thank you to my editor Victoria Godden for truly 'getting' my writing and working so hard to make *Out of Office* something that I'm incredibly proud of.

Thanks to all the people who have contributed their thoughts to this book. Special thanks go to Poorna Bell, Alice Benham, Jessica Berry, Hattie Crisell, Julia Day, Michelle Gately, Robert Hartley, Sinead Latham, Mikhila McDaid, Kirsty Hulse, Vix Meldrew, Kat Nicholls, Sara Tasker and Rachael Watson.

Thank you to all of the friends — both online and offline — who have put up with me constantly complaining about how hard it's been to write this book. I'm very sorry for being a spoilt brat and I appreciate you greatly.

Thanks to anyone who has ever read, shared or talked about my work. Being self-employed is challenging, but the freelance community never fails to provide me with love and support when I need it most.

Thanks to my mum Pauline for always encouraging creativity when I was a child and continuing to cheer me on in every way possible. Thanks to my dad, Alex, for teaching me that working hard and being a nice person are both equally important for a successful freelance career. Thanks to Stuart and Colin for always supporting me in each new endeavour.

Finally, the biggest thanks goes to my husband Joe. Thank you for giving me the space and confidence to try out this freelancing thing and holding my hand along the way. You believed I was capable long before I ever did.

ENDNOTES

1 Oxfordlearnersdictionaries.com, (2020). *Definition of freelance adjective* from the Oxford Advanced Learner›s Dictionary. [online] Available at: <https://www. oxfordlearnersdictionaries.com/definition/english/ freelance_1> [Accessed 25 Mar 2020].

2 Upwork.com, (2019). *Freelancing in America 2019.* [online] Available at: <https://adquiro-content-prod. s3-us-west-1.amazonaws.com/documents/19-0919_ r3_Freelancing+in+America+2019+Infographic. pdf>[Accessed 25 Mar 2020].

3 Payoneer.com, (2019). *The Global Gig-Economy Index.* [online] Available at: <https://pubs.payoneer.com/ images/q2_global_freelancing_index.pdf> [Accessed 25 Mar 2020].

4 Payoneer.com, (2018). *The Payoneer Freelancer Income Survey.* [online] Available at: <https://www.payoneer. com/downloads/freelancer-income-report-2018.pdf> [Accessed 25 Mar 2020].

5 Jenkins, K. (2017). *Exploring The UK Freelance Workforce In 2016.* [online] Available at: <https://www.ipse. co.uk/uploads/assets/uploaded/de84dfb7-283a-4c26-ba446f95f5547c1f.pdf> [Accessed 25 Mar 2020].

6 Jenkins, K. (2017). *Exploring The UK Freelance Workforce In 2016*. [online] Available at: <https://www.ipse. co.uk/uploads/assets/uploaded/de84dfb7-283a-4c26-ba446f95f5547c1f.pdf> [Accessed 25 Mar 2020].

7 nwlc.org, (2013). *It Shouldn't Be a Heavy Lift: fair treatment for pregnant workers.* [online] Available at: <https://nwlc.org/ wp-content/uploads/2015/08/pregnant_workers.pdf> [Accessed 25 Mar 2020].

8 Equalityhumanrights.com, (2015). *Pregnancy And Maternity Discrimination Forces Thousands Of New Mothers Out Of Their Jobs.* [online] Available at: <https:// www.equalityhumanrights.com/en/our-work/news/ pregnancy-and-maternity-discrimination-forces-thousands-new-mothers-out-their-jobs> [Accessed 25 Mar 2020].

9 Codrea-Rado, A. (2019. *Why Women Are Driving Self-Employment Figures.* [online] Available at: <https://www. refinery29.com/en-gb/2019/07/236272/how-to-go-freelance> [Accessed 25 Mar 2020].

10 Smith, S. (2019). The 10 Highest-Paid Jobs You Can Do From Home. *The Telegraph.* [online] Available at: <https://www.telegraph.co.uk/education-and-careers/0/10-highest-paid-jobs-can-do-home/> [Accessed 25 Mar 2020].

11 upwork.com, (2019). *Sixth annual "Freelancing in America" study finds that more people than ever see freelancing as a long-term career path.* [online] Available at: <https://www.upwork. com/press/2019/10/03/freelancing-in-america-2019/> [Accessed 25 Mar 2020].

12 Ons.gov.uk, (2018). *Trends in self-employment in the UK: Analysing the characteristics, income and wealth of the self-employed.* [online] Available at: <https://

www.ons.gov.uk/employmentandlabourmarket/
peopleinwork/employmentandemployeetypes/articles/
trendsinselfemploymentintheuk/2018-02-07> [Accessed
25 Mar 2020].

13 Regus.co.uk, (2019). *The IWG Global Workplace Survey:
Welcome to Generation Flex — the employee power shift.*
[online] Available at: <http://assets.regus.com/pdfs/
iwg-workplace-survey/iwg-workplace-survey-2019.pdf>
[Accessed 25 Mar 2020].

14 Smith, A. (2017). *Working 8 to 4 - what a way to make a
living.* [online] Available at: <https://yougov.co.uk/
topics/politics/articles-reports/2017/11/13/9-5-two-
thirds-working-brits-would-prefer-work-day> [Accessed
25 Mar 2020].

15 Horton, H. (2018). No more working 9 to 5? Vast
majority of Britons now work different hours, study
shows. *The Telegraph.* [online] Available at: <https://
www.telegraph.co.uk/news/2018/08/21/no-working-
9-5-vast-majority-britons-now-work-different-hours/>
[Accessed 25 Mar 2020].

16 Iwgplc.com, (2019). *The IWG Global Workplace Survey:
Welcome to Generation Flex — the employee power shift.*
[online] Available at: <http://assets.regus.com/pdfs/
iwg-workplace-survey/iwg-workplace-survey-2019.pdf>
[Accessed 25 Mar 2020].

17 Nguyen, S. (2017). Results-only work environment
(ROWE). *Workplace Psychology.* [online] Available at:
<https://workplacepsychology.net/2017/01/04/results-
only-work-environment-rowe/> [Accessed 25 Mar
2020].

18 Booth, B. (2018). The future of jobs won't be about
9-to-5 office hours, as power shifts to millennial leaders.

CNBC. [online] Available at: <https://www.cnbc.com/2018/11/14/companies-wont-get-away-with-forcing-9-to-5-workdays-in-the-future-.html> [Accessed 25 Mar 2020].

19 Wheatley, D. (2017). Autonomy in the workplace has positive effects on well-being and job satisfaction, study finds. *Science Daily*. [online] Available at: <https://www.sciencedaily.com/releases/2017/04/170424215501.htm> [Accessed 25 Mar 2020].

20 Gawrych, C. (2019). *What Your Employees Worry about Most in the Workplace HR Advisor Daily*. [online] Available at: <https://hrdailyadvisor.blr.com/2019/03/04/what-your-employees-worry-about-most-in-the-workplace/> [Accessed 25 Mar 2020].

21 equalityhumanrights.com, (2016). *Pregnancy and Maternity-Related Discrimination and Disadvantage: Experience of Mothers*. [online] Available at: <https://www.equalityhumanrights.com/sites/default/files/mothers_report_-_bis-16-146-pregnancy-and-maternity-related-discrimination-and-disadvantage-experiences-of-mothers_1.pdf> [Accessed 25 Mar 2020].

22 Regus.co.uk, (2019). *The IWG Global Workplace Survey: Welcome to Generation Flex — the employee power shift*. [online] Available at: <http://assets.regus.com/pdfs/iwg-workplace-survey/iwg-workplace-survey-2019.pdf> [Accessed 25 Mar 2020].

23 Ons.gov.uk, (2018). *Trends in self-employment in the UK: Analysing the characteristics, income and wealth of the self-employed*. [online] Available at: <https://www.ons.gov.uk/employmentandlabourmarket/peopleinwork/employmentandemployeetypes/articles/trendsinselfemploymentintheuk/2018-02-07> [Accessed 25 Mar 2020].

24 Upwork.com, (2019). *Sixth annual "Freelancing in America" study finds that more people than ever see freelancing as a long-term career path.* [online] Available at: <https://www.upwork.com/press/2019/10/03/freelancing-in-america-2019/> [Accessed 25 Mar 2020].

25 Ipse.co.uk, (2019). *Making Self-Employment Work for Disabled People.* [online] Available at: <https://www.ipse.co.uk/resource/making-self-employment-work-for-disabled-people.html> [Accessed 25 Mar 2020].

26 Molina, B. (2018). How do astronauts poop in space? NASA astronaut Peggy Whitson explains. *USA Today.* [online] Available at: <https://eu.usatoday.com/story/news/nation-now/2018/05/30/how-do-astronauts-poop-space-nasa-astronaut-peggy-whitson-explains/654898002/> [Accessed 25 Mar 2020].

27 Sakulku, J. (2011). The Impostor Phenomenon. *The Journal of Behavioral Science.* [online] Available at: <https://so06.tci-thaijo.org/index.php/IJBS/article/view/521> [Accessed 25 Mar 2020].

28 Ipse.co.uk, (2019). *Rising numbers of female self-employed show "freelancing is a feminist issue".* [online] Available at: <https://www.ipse.co.uk/ipse-news/news-listing/rising-numbers-female-freelancing-feminist-issue.html> [Accessed 25 Mar 2020].

29 Henley.ac.uk, (2018). *Side hustles contribute £72 billion to UK economy.* [online] Available at: <https://www.henley.ac.uk/news/2018/side-business-is-big-business> [Accessed 25 Mar 2020].

30 Gannon, E. (2019). *Side hustlers aren't just for young people @BBC Breakfast.* [online] Available at: <https://twitter.com/emmagannon/status/1086214235032559616> [Accessed 25 Mar 2020].

31 Gov.uk, (2020). *Register For And File Your Self Assessment Tax Return*. [online] Available at: <https://www.gov.uk/log-in-file-self-assessment-tax-return/register-if-youre-self-employed> [Accessed 23 Mar 2020].

32 Bonnet, S. (2011). The average cost of coworking: two cups of coffee a day. *Desk Mag.* [online] Available at: <http://www.deskmag.com/en/the-average-cost-of-coworking-spaces-survey-218> [Accessed 23 Mar 2020].

33 Ico.org.uk, (2018). *Data Protection Fee*. [online] Available at: <https://ico.org.uk/for-organisations/data-protection-fee/> [Accessed 23 Mar 2020].

34 Gov.uk, (n.d). *Understand your self-assessment tax bill.* [online] Available at: <https://www.gov.uk/understand-self-assessment-bill/payments-on-account> [Accessed 23 Mar 2020].

35 Gov.uk, (n.d). *Vat registration.* [online] Available at: <https://www.gov.uk/vat-registration/when-to-register> [Accessed 23 Mar 2020].

36 Wilks, B. (2019). Freelancers strike back: Saying "no" to free work. *Dinghy.* [online] Available at: <https://getdinghy.com/knowledgebase/freelancers-strike-back-saying-no-to-free-work/> [Accessed 23 Mar 2020].

37 Beingboss.club, (2018). *The Chalkboard Method: A Visual Goal Setting System for Creatives*. [online] Available at: <https://beingboss.club/downloads/worksheets/BeingBoss_ChalkboardMethod.pdf> [Accessed 23 Mar 2020].

38 Godin, S. (2011). *On pricing power.* [online] Available at: <https://seths.blog/2011/02/on-pricing-power/> [Accessed 23 Mar 2020].

39 Rodway, P. Schepman, A. Lambert, J. (2011). *Preferring the One in the Middle: Further Evidence for the Centre-stage Effect.*

[online] Available at: <https://onlinelibrary.wiley.com/doi/abs/10.1002/acp.1812> [Accessed 23 Mar 2020].

40 Freelanceuk.com, (n.d). *How freelancers can avoid late payments*. [online] Available at: <https://www.freelanceuk.com/running_business/automated-invoicing-credit-scores-can-help-freelancers-avoid-late-payments.shtml> [Accessed 23 Mar 2020].

41 Gov.uk, (n.d). *Invoicing and taking payment from customers*. [online] Available at: <https://www.gov.uk/invoicing-and-taking-payment-from-customers/invoices-what-they-must-include> [Accessed 23 Mar 2020].

42 Gov.uk, (n.d). *Invoicing and taking payment from customers*. [online] Available at: <https://www.gov.uk/invoicing-and-taking-payment-from-customers/payment-obligations> [Accessed 23 Mar 2020].

43 Xero.com, (2019). *Business Rewired: The technology and trends shaping the future of small business*. [online] Available at: <https://www.xero.com/content/dam/xero/pdf/Campaign/UK/business-rewired/business-rewired.pdf> [Accessed 23 Mar 2020].

44 Gov.uk, (n.d). *Late commercial payments: charging interest and debt recovery*. [online] Available at: <https://www.gov.uk/late-commercial-payments-interest-debt-recovery> [Accessed 23 Mar 2020].

45 Kratz, G. (2019). Study: Remote Work Productivity and Job Performance. *Flex Jobs*. [online] Available at: <https://www.flexjobs.com/employer-blog/remote-work-productivity-study/> [Accessed 23 Mar 2020].

46 Jepps, C. (2019). *Remote Working*. [online] Available at: <https://www.ipse.co.uk/resource/remote-working.html> [Accessed 23 Mar 2020].

47 Umberson, D. and Karas Montez, J. (2010). Social Relationships and Health: A Flashpoint for Health Policy. *Journal of Health and Social Behavior.* [online] Available at: <https://www.ncbi.nlm.nih.gov/pmc/articles/PMC3150158/> [Accessed 23 Mar 2020].

48 Umberson, D. and Karas Montez, J. (2010). Social Relationships and Health: A Flashpoint for Health Policy. *Journal of Health and Social Behavior.* [online] Available at: <https://www.ncbi.nlm.nih.gov/pmc/articles/PMC3150158/> [Accessed 23 Mar 2020].

49 Antonovsky, A. (1987). *Unraveling the mystery of health: How people manage stress and stay well.* San Francisco, CA, US: Jossey-Bass.

50 Goins, J. (2016). The Three Types Of Relationship Every Creative Person Needs. [online] *Fast Company.* Available at: <https://www.fastcompany.com/3063668/why-creativity-depends-on-your-relationships-as-much-as-your-talent>[Accessed 23 Mar 2020].

51 Franklin, N. (2018). Many UK Freelancers Feel Lonely And Isolated Following Leap To Self-Employment. [online] *Workplace Insight.* Available at: <https://workplaceinsight.net/many-uk-freelancers-feel-lonely-and-isolated-following-leap-to-self-employment/> [Accessed 23 Mar 2020].

52 Franklin, N. (2018). Many UK Freelancers Feel Lonely And Isolated Following Leap To Self-Employment. [online] *Workplace Insight.* Available at: <https://workplaceinsight.net/many-uk-freelancers-feel-lonely-and-isolated-following-leap-to-self-employment/> [Accessed 23 Mar 2020].

53 Morehead, J. (2012). Stanford University's Carol Dweck On The Growth Mindset And Education. *One

Dublin. [online] Available at: <https://onedublin.
org/2012/06/19/stanford-universitys-carol-dweck-on-
the-growth-mindset-and-education/> [Accessed 23 Mar
2020].

54 Garvin, R. (2019). *How Social Networks Influence 74%
Of Shoppers For Their Purchasing Decisions Today.* [online]
Available at: <https://awario.com/blog/how-social-
networks-influence-74-of-shoppers-for-their-purchasing-
decisions-today/> [Accessed 23 Mar 2020].

55 Williams, L. (2018). Laura Jane Williams: ‹Stop
Slagging Off Instagram’. *Red Online.* [online] Available
at: <https://www.redonline.co.uk/red-women/blogs/
a531674/laura-jane-williams-instagram1/> [Accessed
23 Mar 2020].

56 Leapers.co, (2019). *Leapers: Research Study 2019.* [online]
Available at: <https://www.leapers.co/huru>[Accessed
23 Mar 2020].

57 Cockburn, S. (n.d). *Improve Customer Service, Increase
Sales (Infographic).* [online] Available at: <https://
growingsocialbiz.com/improve-customer-service-
increase-sales-infographic/> [Accessed 23 Mar 2020].

58 Hayden, J. (2019). All Day And All Of The Night: Are
Freelancers Night Owls? *Modern Work Magazine.* [online]
Available at: <https://www.modernworkmag.co.uk/are-
freelancers-night-owls/> [Accessed 23 Mar 2020].

59 Hayden, J. (2019). All Day And All Of The Night: Are
Freelancers Night Owls? *Modern Work Magazine.* [online]
Available at: <https://www.modernworkmag.co.uk/are-
freelancers-night-owls/> [Accessed 23 Mar 2020].

60 Gilbert, E. (n.d.). *Thoughts on Writing.* [online] Available
at: <https://www.elizabethgilbert.com/thoughts-on-
writing/> [Accessed 23 Mar 2020].

61 Muttucumaru, A. (2017). Do You Need a 'Power Hour' in Your Day? *Get The Gloss*. [online] Available at: <https://www.getthegloss.com/behind-the-brand/do-you-need-a-power-hour-in-your-day> [Accessed 23 Mar 2020].

62 Santos, G. (2018). 33 Ways to Increase Dopamine to Boost Your Productivity. *Endless Events*. [online] Available at: <https://helloendless.com/10-ways-to-increase-dopamine-to-boost-your-productivity/> [Accessed 23 Mar 2020].

63 Weinschenk, S. (2012). The True Cost Of Multi-Tasking. *Psychology Today*. [online] Available at: <https://www.psychologytoday.com/gb/blog/brain-wise/201209/the-true-cost-multi-tasking> [Accessed 23 Mar 2020].

64 Rothman, A.J. (2000). Toward a theory-based analysis of behavioral maintenance, *Health Psychology*. [online] Available at: <https://experts.umn.edu/en/publications/toward-a-theory-based-analysis-of-behavioral-maintenance> [Accessed 23 Mar 2020].

65 Dai, H., Milkman, K.L., Riis, J. (2014). The Fresh Start Effect: Temporal Landmarks Motivate Aspirational Behavior, *Management Science*. [online] Available at: <https://pubsonline.informs.org/doi/abs/10.1287/mnsc.2014.1901> [Accessed 23 Mar 2020].

66 O'Brien, K. (2017). Creativity meets collaboration as marketers find new ways to work in a mobile world at Advertising Week. *The Drum*. [online] Available at: <https://www.thedrum.com/news/2017/09/26/creativity-meets-collaboration-marketers-find-new-ways-work-mobile-world-advertising> [Accessed 23 Mar 2020].

67 Greenberg, M. (2016). Why Some Stress Is Good for You. *Psychology Today.* [online] Available at: <https://www.psychologytoday.com/gb/blog/the-mindful-self-express/201612/why-some-stress-is-good-you> [Accessed 23 Mar 2020].

68 Seery, M., Holman, E. and Silver, R. (2010). Whatever does not kill us: Cumulative lifetime adversity, vulnerability, and resilience. *Journal of Personality and Social Psychology.* [online] Available at: <https://www.ncbi.nlm.nih.gov/pubmed/20939649> [Accessed 23 Mar 2020].

69 www.who.int, (2019). *Burn-out an "occupational phenomenon": International Classification of Diseases.* [online] Available at: <https://www.who.int/mental_health/evidence/burn-out/en/> [Accessed 23 Mar 2020].

70 Leapers.co, (2019). *Leapers: Research Study 2019.* [online] Available at: <https://www.leapers.co/huru> [Accessed 23 Mar 2020].

71 Sciencedaily.com, (2018). Running helps brain stave off effects of chronic stress: Exercise protects vital memory and learning functions. *Science Daily* [online] Available at: <www.sciencedaily.com/releases/2018/02/180214093823.htm> [Accessed 23 Mar 2020].

72 Ratey, J.J. (2019). Can exercise help treat anxiety? *Harvard Health Blog.* [online] Available at: <https://www.health.harvard.edu/blog/can-exercise-help-treat-anxiety-2019102418096> [Accessed 23 Mar 2020].

73 Hwang, J., Wang, L., Siever, J., Medico, T. and Jones, C. (2018). *Loneliness and social isolation among older adults in a community exercise program: a qualitative study.* [online] Available at: <https://www.ncbi.nlm.nih.gov/pubmed/29543517> [Accessed 23 Mar 2020].

74 Goldacre, B. (2007). What's wrong with Gillian McKeith? *The Guardian*. [online] Available at: <https://www.theguardian.com/media/2007/feb/12/advertising.food> [Accessed 23 Mar 2020].

75 Banskota, S., Ghia, J. and Khan, W. (2019). Serotonin in the gut: Blessing or a curse. *Science Direct*. [online] Available at: <https://www.sciencedirect.com/science/article/abs/pii/S0300908418301652> [Accessed 23 Mar 2020].

76 McIntosh, J. (2018). What is serotonin and what does it do? *Medical News Today*. [online] Available at: <https://www.medicalnewstoday.com/kc/serotonin-facts-232248> [Accessed 23 Mar 2020].

77 Ernst, J. (2010). Five minutes in the green can boost self esteem. *Reuters*. [online] Available at: <https://www.reuters.com/article/us-mental-health-green-idUSTRE6401Y620100502> [Accessed 23 Mar 2020].

78 Magee, A. (2016). Why fresh air is the best medicine. *The Telegraph*. [online] Available at: <https://www.telegraph.co.uk/health-fitness/body/why-fresh-air-is-the-best-medicine/> [Accessed 23 Mar 2020].

79 Sciencedaily.com, (2016). Creative activities promote day-to-day wellbeing. *Science Daily*. [online] Available at: <https://www.sciencedaily.com/releases/2016/11/161123183914.htm> [Accessed 23 Mar 2020].

80 Ipse.co.uk, (2019). *Taking Time Off As A Freelancer*. [online] Available at: <https://www.ipse.co.uk/resource/taking-time-off-as-a-freelancer.html> [Accessed 23 Mar 2020].

81 Ipse.co.uk, (2019). *Taking Time Off As A Freelancer*. [online] Available at: <https://www.ipse.co.uk/resource/taking-time-off-as-a-freelancer.html> [Accessed 23 Mar 2020].

USEFUL RESOURCES

FURTHER READING

Company of One: Why Staying Small is the Next Big Thing for Business by Paul Jarvis

Quiet: The Power of Introverts in a World That Can't Stop Talking by Susan Cain

The Multi-Hyphen Life: Work Less, Create More, and Design a Life That Works for You by Emma Gannon

The Future is Freelance by Kirsty Hulse

The Working Woman's Handbook: Ideas, Insights, and Inspiration for a Successful Creative Career by Phoebe Lovatt

Hype Yourself: A no-nonsense DIY PR toolkit for small businesses by Lucy Werner

Work Simply: Embracing The Power of Your Personal Productivity Style by Carson Tate

WEBSITES

www.ipse.co.uk
www.freelancelifestyle.co.uk
www.gov.uk
www.worknotes.co.uk

ONLINE COMMUNITIES

www.growglow.co
www.independentgirlscollective.com
www.jesswho.co.uk/the-co-working-club

PODCASTS

Being Boss
Being Freelance
Ctrl Alt Delete
Freelance Feels
No Bull Business Women
She Can. She Did.
Squiggly Careers
Starting The Conversation

TriggerHub.org is one of the most elite and scientifically proven forms of mental health intervention

Trigger Publishing is the leading independent mental health and wellbeing publisher in the UK and US. Clinical and scientific research conducted by assistant professor Dr Kristin Kosyluk and her highly acclaimed team in the Department of Mental Health Law & Policy at the University of South Florida (USF), as well as complementary research by her peers across the US, has independently verified the power of lived experience as a core component in achieving mental health prosperity. Specifically, the lived experiences contained within our bibliotherapeutic books are intrinsic elements in reducing stigma, making those with poor mental health feel less alone, providing the privacy they need to heal, ensuring they know the essential steps to kick-start their own journeys to recovery, and providing hope and inspiration when they need it most.

Delivered through TriggerHub, our unique online portal and accompanying smartphone app, we make our library of bibliotherapeutic titles and other vital resources accessible to individuals and organizations anywhere, at any time and with complete privacy, a crucial element of recovery. As such, TriggerHub is the primary recommendation across the UK and US for the delivery of lived experiences.

At Trigger Publishing and TriggerHub, we proudly lead the way in making the unseen become seen. We are dedicated to humanizing mental health, breaking stigma and challenging outdated societal values to create real action and impact. Find out more about our world-leading work with lived experience and bibliotherapy via triggerhub.org, or by joining us on:

- @triggerhub_
- @triggerhub.org
- @triggerhub_

ABOUT SHAWMIND

A proportion of profits from the sale of all Trigger books go to their sister charity, Shawmind, also founded by Adam Shaw and Lauren Callaghan. The charity aims to ensure that everyone has access to mental health resources whenever they need them.

You can find out more about the work Shawmind do by visiting their website: shawmind.org or joining them on

Twitter @shawmind_

Facebook @shawmindUK

Instagram @shawmind_

Your Local Mental Health & Wellbeing Charity

Printed in the USA
CPSIA information can be obtained
at www.ICGtesting.com
JSHW03170714O824
68134JS00038B/3562

9 781837 962884